Table of Contents

BRICK BY BRICK

My Journey Through Real Estate and Beyond

Dr. Kettaki Kasbekar

INDIA • SINGAPORE • MALAYSIA

ISBN
Hardcase 979-8-89673-450-5
Paperback 979-8-89632-977-0

Born Under a Blessed Star

Lao Tzu once said, *"A journey of a thousand miles begins with a single step."* I've always felt a connection to these words because they remind me that every journey, no matter how long or unpredictable, has a starting point. As I sit down to share my own journey, filled with highs, lows, and plenty of twists, I can't help but reflect on where it all began. For me, that first step was taken on a very special day, a day filled with both personal meaning and celebration: Ganesh Jayanti.

In India, Lord Ganesh is cherished like no other. He's the god we turn to for wisdom, for good fortune, and for opening doors to new possibilities. For generations, families have kept his idol at home, trusting in his ability to remove obstacles and bring success to their pursuits. It's not just a belief—it's a bond. People feel his presence in their lives, guiding them, protecting them, and helping them through life's twists and turns.

When it's time to honor Lord Ganesh, especially during festivals and life's important milestones, devotion fills the air. People gather with deep reverence, offering prayers and observing fasts, and many families perform a Ganesh Yagna, a sacred ritual with offerings to the fire, asking for his blessings. On Ganesh Jayanti, his birth anniversary, the celebrations are especially heartfelt. For those who pray to him, Ganesh isn't just a god; he's a symbol of wisdom, a bringer of good luck, and a guide to new beginnings.

It was within this setting that I entered the world. My father named me Chaitali - a name that means "blessed with a good memory" or "having a sharp memory," reflecting intelligence and a strong connection to the earth.

My grandmother lovingly cradled me, already knowing the name she would give me - Durvi. To my grandmother, the name Durvi carried a deeper meaning. Durvi is connected to the sacred Durva grass we offer to Lord Ganesha, a symbol of strength, resilience, and the ability to endure. From the very start, she believed that this name would guide me through whatever life had in store. It's funny, but when I think of that day, I can almost see my grandmother looking at me as if she already knew that the path ahead wouldn't always be easy, but it would be one marked by resilience. It was like she had given me a small piece of destiny wrapped in those five letters.

As I grew up, my grandmother remained a central figure in my life. She lived with us, and her presence was an integral part of my childhood. She was more than just a grandmother; she was my teacher, my storyteller, my best friend, my philosopher and my source of wisdom. Some of my earliest memories are of her sitting by my side, teaching me little life lessons, often without saying much at all. I learned so much from simply watching her: her quiet strength, her unwavering patience, and her belief that there's always a way forward, no matter how hard the path seems.

I can still picture her in our living room, her soft hands busy with some task while she gently talked about life, family, and the importance of staying grounded. Her wisdom wasn't always in grand speeches but in the small, everyday moments. And then, of course, there were her bedtime stories. In her stories, Durvi was always a bold heroine—at times a princess, at other times a queen, and at times a fierce warrior. I remember lying under the blankets, listening intently, completely captivated by the adventures she would spin. In one story, Durvi was a fearless queen defending her kingdom against invaders with nothing but her wit and courage. In another, she was a daring princess, saving her people from disaster. Each story painted Durvi as someone who was strong and resilient, and each time my grandmother spoke that name, I felt it belonged to me in a way I couldn't yet fully understand.

Those stories stayed with me. The next day, I would go to school, head held high, proudly proclaiming to my friends, "My name is Durvi," as if I was announcing something important. I even remember a few times when I'd pretend I was the princess or the queen from the stories, imagining that one day, I would face my own challenges with the same kind of strength.

My childhood felt like a little slice of heaven. I was cherished and pampered by everyone in the family, surrounded by constant love and support. Academically, I thrived, thanks to my well-educated family, who always encouraged me to do my best. In school, I wasn't just known among classmates but also recognized by teachers and even the principal, who saw my dedication and achievements.

I had a close circle of friends with whom I shared countless memories, and I was naturally drawn to the lively world of cultural activities. I participated in nearly every event our school held—drama, dance, singing, sports—you name it. Being in the limelight felt second nature, and these experiences enriched my early years, building my confidence and shaping who I was becoming.

It was a time filled with joy, learning, and endless opportunities. It instilled in me a strong sense of belonging, along with a deep love for academics and community, two things that would guide me throughout my life.

For most kids, Diwali is often the favorite festival, but for me, it was always Ganesh Chaturthi. The excitement of the ten-day Ganapati festival was something I eagerly awaited all year. Each year, I would join my father and brothers for the special task of selecting our Ganapati idol, a moment that filled me with pure joy.

A Curious Mind

As the years passed, I grew into both names - Durvi and Chaitali. Sometimes, I was mischievous and a little naughty, and sometimes, I was the pampered child my family doted on. But most of the time, you could find me with my nose buried deep in a newspaper. I had this morning routine before school that became almost sacred to me. Every day, like clockwork, I would get lost in the pages of *Sakaal*, our Marathi newspaper, flipping through it from the front to the children's supplement. My mom would often have to almost drag me away to get me ready for school on time, shaking her head at my little obsession.

But as soon as I came home and finished my homework, I'd head straight to my dad. I'd look up at him with an eager smile, and without fail, he'd retrieve the newspaper for me, handing it over with a knowing look. The first thing I'd do was turn straight to the Sudoku puzzle I'd left unfinished in the morning, determined to crack it before dinner.

After a while, though, it wasn't just the Sudoku that had my attention. I began exploring the other sections, leafing through articles and absorbing every headline, every word, with this unshakable fascination. It was as if each sentence was a tiny piece of magic, something that could transport me to different worlds beyond our quiet home. Before I knew it, I was devouring the entire paper, cover to cover, feeling like I was part of every story, every event that unfolded.

Soon, I was voracious for any kind of reading material. I'd read anything I could get my hands on. Give me a book, a pamphlet, or even a flyer, and I'd dive in, soaking up whatever information it held. Looking back, leaving me with reading material was like leaving a kid alone in a candy store; I couldn't help myself. I remember when we bought our first color TV. It was a big day for us. The TV came with this thick Onida manual that everyone in the family tried to read but quickly set aside out of boredom. Not me. I sat there, flipping through each page of the manual, taking in every word and diagram. By the time I was done, I knew exactly how the remote worked, what each button did, and how to bring that screen to life.

When I proudly told my brothers and my father how to operate the TV, they laughed at first, thinking it was one of my little quirks. But then I clicked the right buttons, and when that screen lit up with colorful images for the first time, they all cheered. My father even lifted me up, pride and joy written all over his face. It was such a simple moment, but to me, it felt like I'd unlocked something big, like knowledge was this magical thing that could make moments like these happen.

My love for reading gradually became something of a reputation in our warm and close-knit neighborhood. The school I went to was semi-English medium, but that didn't limit me. I was always on the lookout for more stories in any language I could find. One of the most welcoming families around us was a Catholic family nearby. They had a son who attended a CBSE school, and his books were like hidden treasures to me. Whenever I could, I would borrow them, eager to dive into whatever new world those pages held. I even found myself captivated by the Bible, which I read with their family.

This family was always kind and supportive, never questioning why I was so eager to borrow books. Instead, they would smile, often remarking on my voracious appetite for reading. Looking back, I'm deeply grateful for their encouragement, along with the support from my own family. These gentle nudges played a crucial role in shaping who I was becoming, allowing me to indulge my curiosity without reservation.

As a young child, I was known for being quite naughty and exceptionally strong-minded, with a resolve that appeared in all my actions. Even with my playful nature, there were times when unforeseen patience and endurance would emerge. I was in 6th grade, right in the midst of my final exams, when I began to feel intense stomach pain. The pain was so severe that concentrating on my studies seemed almost unattainable.

Worried, my father brought me to the doctor, who promptly suggested a sonography to identify the cause of the discomfort.

The diagnosis was definite and critical—I had appendicitis, and the doctor recommended prompt surgery to avoid any complications. He recommended that I be taken to the hospital immediately, even if it risked my remaining tests. My dad, ever encouraging, confirmed that my well-being was the priority and that the tests could be completed at a later time. Yet, even at such a young age, I remained steadfast. I turned to my father and said, "No, I'll complete my exams first, then we can head to the hospital." I was resolute in completing my exams, despite the pain, before addressing the surgery. My father, surprised at first by my determination, ultimately honored my choice. Thus, I returned, finished both tests, and only then permitted myself to undergo the surgery.

Reflecting on it, I realized that the situation revealed not only my tenacious nature but also my commitment to completing what I had begun, regardless of the challenges. It's a quality that has stayed with me all my life, steering me through difficulties and reminding me of the power that even a youthful heart can possess. As time went on, I found myself immersed in the works of Marathi author P.L. Deshpande and the writing of Shobhaa De. I really connected with Deshpande's humor and sharp observations about society when I was growing up. The way he makes everyday life feel so extraordinary, filled with laughter and warmth, really left a lasting impression on me. I admired Shobhaa De's boldness; her way of writing about women's lives and their experiences with such frankness felt empowering, especially as I was beginning to think about what my own future might hold.

Those authors, along with the endless books I was fortunate enough to stumble upon, played such an important role in shaping my view of the world. They gave me perspectives I wouldn't have had otherwise. With all the worlds I was discovering through books, I began to find inspiration in real figures, too, people whose stories were as powerful as anything I'd read in fiction. One of the most formidable influences for me was Indira Gandhi. I remember the day when she was assassinated. At the time, I didn't fully grasp who she was or why her life mattered so deeply to the country. But as I grew older and read more about her, her journey began to feel familiar, almost like those stories my grandmother would tell me at bedtime.

Indira Gandhi's life was one of triumph in the face of unimaginable loss. She endured personal tragedies, lost family, faced the challenges of political power, and, most of all, constantly pushed forward in a world where the odds were rarely in her favor. She had faced opposition, criticism, and adversity at every turn, yet she seemed to rise above it all with a fierce resolve. I remember one of her quotes that struck me deeply: "You cannot shake hands with a clenched fist." I would go back to that line often, thinking about how it captured her resilience and her firm yet open approach to the world.

Her story inspired me in many ways, especially in learning to be self-reliant, embracing simplicity, and always choosing action over hesitation. She had walked through a male-dominated world with her head held high, and she left a mark that was impossible to ignore.

Inspired by her, I found myself drawn to helping others, even at a young age. My grandmother was very involved in our community, always lending a hand to people in need. She would often help neighbor mothers of soldiers and young women who had lost their spouses in handling the process of securing pensions or benefits. I would tag along to those meetings, watching her work patiently, guiding them through the form, and explaining each step in her gentle way. She was a steady hand and a source of comfort to these women, and I could see how much her support meant to them. There was something deeply fulfilling about being part of those efforts. My grandmother would smile proudly whenever I managed to assist with even the smallest tasks, and it made me feel like I was contributing to something important.

Another important inspiration during my childhood came from a place most Indian kids can relate to: the world of films. Growing up in India, it's hard to overlook the influence Bollywood has on us.

In our house, Sundays were special. After a week full of school and work, we'd all settle down in front of the TV. Those days were filled with excitement, especially when Doordarshan was showing an Amitabh Bachchan movie. His films were a family favorite, and whenever he appeared on screen, I was hooked. There was something about the way he brought his characters to life that made me forget everything else. Watching him, I felt like I was part of the drama and the grandeur unfolding before my eyes.

One Sunday stands out vividly. We all gathered in the living room as the familiar Doordarshan logo flashed on the screen, and soon enough, Trishul's opening credits rolled in. I had seen several of Bachchan's films before, but there was something about *Trishul* that felt different. As the film started, I could feel the excitement bubbling inside me. The moment Amitabh Bachchan appeared on screen—his towering presence, the way he carried himself—it was as if the whole room froze, and all eyes were on him.

My parents and brothers were equally captivated, but for me, it felt personal. I must have been barely seven or eight years old, yet I was already a full-fledged Amitabh Bachchan fan. And as I watched him that night, playing the fearless Vijay in *Trishul*, it felt like I was witnessing something special. Even my father noticed how engrossed I was, occasionally glancing over and smiling, perhaps realizing that his little girl was just as thrilled by Bachchan's magic as he was.

Later that week, when we had guests over, my dad nudged me with a grin and whispered, "Come on, recite one of Amitabh's dialogues." I didn't need much convincing. Since watching *Trishul*, one line had become my favorite: "Main paanch lakh ka sauda karne aaya hoon ... aur meri jeb mein paanch phooti kaudiyaan bhi nahin hai." With the guests' attention turned towards me, I stood up, channeling all the confidence and intensity I had absorbed from the screen.

As I delivered the line, I tried to mimic Amitabh's commanding tone and stern gaze. The guests would laugh, sometimes in surprise at how seriously I took the role, but their applause always made me feel like I had done Amitabh justice in some small way. Each time I said those words, it felt like I was stepping into another world, a world where I could be as fearless and bold as the characters I admired.

This love for Amitabh Bachchan, for Trishul, and for the art of performance itself slowly began to awaken something in me: the artist. Beyond studies, I found myself drawn to extracurricular activities, particularly theater. It was interesting how art and performance could combine with social messages, leaving a lasting impression. School plays and skits became a space where I could express myself while also understanding deeper messages about the world around me.

One such experience was when I got the chance to perform in a Marathi dance-drama called *Durga Zali Gauri*. *Durga Zali Gauri* was a Marathi dance-drama that told the story of a young, entitled princess named Durga who went through a transformative journey, eventually evolving into Gauri, a compassionate figure filled with empathy and understanding. The tale followed her as she started off blaming others for her problems, protected by her royal privilege, with her every whim indulged by her parents, the king and queen. One day, though, everything changed. The king, refusing to appease her anymore, left her to confront her own choices. In a moment of rebellion, Durga left the palace, setting off on a path of self-discovery. Along the way, she encountered nature, mingled with the common people, and gradually learned the value of hard work and compassion. By the end, Durga transformed completely, becoming Gauri- her journey to humility and love is now complete.

I remember being cast in this play in 8th grade. The story felt so personal to me. As the only daughter in a close-knit family, spoiled by both my dad and grandma, I really connected with Durga's initial sense of entitlement and her journey toward maturity. It mirrored my own growth, and I was determined to bring that experience to life on stage. The day of the performance arrived, and I could feel my nerves setting in. I stood backstage, my heart racing, hands clammy, running through my lines and steps in my head. When my turn came, I took a deep breath, stepped into the lights, and let the character of Durga take over.

By the time the final scene came, when Durga transformed into Gauri, I felt a surge of something hard to put into words. It was a mixture of liberation, relief, and pride. The applause filled the room, but what stayed with me most was the feeling that this story, Durga's journey and her growth, was a piece of my own journey.

The First Dream

Over the years, much like Durga's journey in the play, my own life began to reveal its twists and turns. By the time I was approaching my board exams, I had a clear vision of what I wanted to be. It was a dream that had been growing within me for years. Inspired by my grandmother's dedication to service, my family's humility, and my own insatiable curiosity, I realized I wanted to become a doctor.

My family has always been my steady source of support, standing by me in every decision I've taken except real estate. Since we were young, my father taught us the importance of mutual respect and honest communication. He ensured that we were part of every family decision, whether significant or minor, fostering a home where every opinion was valued and acknowledged. This atmosphere fostered numerous constructive discussions—particularly when our views conflicted—but these interactions showed us the importance of critical thinking and boosted our confidence in making well-informed decisions. Reflecting on these experiences, I see that they not only influenced our decision-making skills but also fostered a profound sense of independence and resilience that I carry throughout every aspect of my life.

Every evening, as I settled down at my study table with books stacked high around me, I'd take a moment to imagine the future I was working towards. I would see myself in a crisp white coat, a stethoscope draped around my neck, deeply immersed in medical textbooks. This vision kept me motivated during those long nights of studying. It was the image I clung to during moments of fatigue when exams felt overwhelming and when doubt began to creep in. I kept reminding myself: this is what you're working for.

When I finally completed my board exams, the waiting period for the results felt like a test of patience in itself. My dream of stepping into the world of medicine felt so close, yet everything hinged on the results. And then, the day arrived: my results were out. The exhilaration of that moment is still fresh in my memory. I remember the way my heart raced as I checked the marks, the joy that surged through me when I saw that I had secured a seat in medicine. It felt like all those nights of studying, of visualizing myself as a doctor, were finally paying off.

I was accepted into a prestigious medical college, and it seemed like the start of a grand adventure. I moved into the hostel, full of optimism and ready to take on the rigorous demands of medical studies. For a brief two months, life was everything I had hoped it would be. But then, abruptly, it all came undone. Life, unpredictable as it is, threw a wrench in my well-laid plans. What happened next still haunts me like a nightmare.

I can still recall that evening as if it happened yesterday. I was at the hostel, having dinner and talking with friends. Out of the blue, the hostel manager approached me and said, "You have a phone call." Back then, there were no cell phones or pagers, making it uncommon to receive a call. I believed it was merely an ordinary call, but I was completely mistaken.

As I picked up the phone, I sensed that something was really, really off. My heart dropped, and it seemed as if my entire world was flipping over. The person in charge must have noticed my surprise as she immediately offered to drive me home. During the drive, I kept assuming it would just be a brief stay, perhaps a month, and I would quickly return to complete my studies. I had no idea that I was departing from the hostel for the final time.

In the days that came after, I attempted to comprehend what had occurred, yet inside, I realized I couldn't return. It was a choice I made for my family, and while it shattered my heart, I didn't see any alternative option. I dedicated all my efforts to my aspiration of becoming a doctor, giving up a lot to chase it. However, at that time, I needed to set my aspirations aside.

It was distressing. I recall feeling conflicted, yet family was everything to me, and I couldn't abandon them. Therefore, I decided to abandon the dream I had invested my heart in, even though that choice would linger with me for eternity. Many of my relatives are doctors and engineers, so when I chose to move away from a career in medicine, I faced numerous questions from both myself and others. "What comes next?" seemed like a large, ambiguous inquiry looming above me, leaving me with doubt.

A neighbor observed my difficulties and urged me to think about pathology, recommending that I enroll in the medical college in town. It seemed like a rescue at a moment when I was uncertain about which path to follow. Having achieved a good score in my board exams, I felt assured about gaining admission, and my academic abilities led me to believe I could easily make up for the three or four months of classes I had missed.

Yet, in the midst of that despair, I discovered a resilience within myself. Something inside me refused to let me collapse under the weight of my disappointment. Instead of succumbing to frustration and sorrow,

I chose to adapt. Making the decision wasn't easy, but I redirected my focus to pathology.

I began to explore a new path in pathology. Even as I made this choice, I knew that it wasn't the dream I had nurtured for so long. This path was a compromise, a plan B, but at that moment, it was what I had to do.

Life has a way of disrupting even the best-laid plans, and what happened next still feels like a nightmare. I vividly remember that dark day—black, not just for me but for my entire family. Unexpected family circumstances turned my world upside down. My top priority, the dream of becoming a doctor that I had held onto for so long, suddenly slipped out of my grasp. I was devastated, and the weight of disappointment was crushing, as if the future I had envisioned was slipping through my fingers faster than I could hold on.

But amidst the despair, I found strength within myself. Something deep inside wouldn't let me crumble entirely. Instead of letting frustration and sadness consume me, I decided to adapt. It wasn't an easy decision, but I chose to shift my focus to pathology. I knew this wasn't the dream I had nurtured all these years; it was a compromise, a Plan B. It didn't ignite the same passion, but it was the path I needed to follow at that moment. And while it wasn't what I had originally planned for myself, it was still an opportunity to build a meaningful career—one that would shape the person I was becoming. In those uncertain years, as I adjusted to this new direction, life around me found its own rhythm. My family, too, began to settle.

At first, the work absorbed me. The precision of the lab and the methodical patterns of study all had a certain order in which I could lose myself. But as the weeks stretched into months, a faint unease began to creep in, like the distant hum of an uninvited thought. Each slide I examined and each case I studied carried with it a growing sense of detachment. It wasn't immediate, more like a shadow gathering at the edges of my vision. I was doing the work and meeting the demands, but something essential was missing. The realization grew gradually, like water seeping into cracks, until I could no longer ignore it. Pathology, while necessary at that moment, wasn't where I belonged.

I started noticing that I was drifting away from my studies, taking breaks I couldn't really explain. Each time I stepped away, I felt a pang of guilt, but there was also a sense of relief that I didn't have to be there. I kept telling myself it was just a phase and that I'd get back on track soon, but deep down, I knew something else was going on.

The more I took a step back, the clearer things became. I realized I missed that drive and a sense of purpose that used to motivate everything I did. Each day made it obvious that my true passion wasn't in the lab. Deep down, I felt a longing for something greater, something that stretched beyond those walls. It was like my mind and heart were shouting, "There's more out there for you!" And for the first time, I was finally ready to listen.

As I listened, a flood of questions rushed over me. What was this "more"? Where would it lead? The lab, once a place of comfort and routine, now felt constricting, unable to contain the growing desire inside me. I realized I was at a crossroads, a moment that would shape my career and who I really was. Despite the uncertainty, I felt a strange calmness, like the quiet before a storm. I was ready to leave the familiar behind and search for a path that would reignite my passion for life. But where would I go? What would taking that leap actually look like?

Breaking New Ground

A Shift in Passion

Pursuing a career in pathology was more of an adjustment than a passion for me. I was initially drawn to the white coat—the prestige and the sense of purpose that came with the medical profession. But deep down, I knew it wasn't where my heart truly lay. The decision to study pathology felt like a practical choice rather than something I was genuinely excited about. After graduating, I joined a prestigious diagnostic center in Pune, a renowned name in the field. I performed exceptionally well academically and was awarded a Gold Medal for securing the highest marks at one of the top medical institutes in Pune.

But despite these achievements, something felt off. I couldn't shake the feeling that I was following a path that didn't resonate with who I was or what I really wanted. The weight of that inner dissatisfaction began to bear down on me. Each morning, getting up for work felt heavier than the day before. I started taking leaves, telling myself it was just temporary, that I needed a break, but deep down, I knew the truth—I had lost the motivation. The drive, the excitement that once fueled me, had faded. Pathology, once something I thought would define me, now felt like a cage. Each step I took felt more burdensome than the last. It wasn't the exhaustion of work itself—it was emotional.

I was drained and disconnected, and that terrified me. At first, I tried to make the best of it. I convinced myself that I could push through this growing detachment. But the more I stayed, the more alienated I became from myself. It was like I was going through the motions but not truly living them. For someone who had always taken pride in giving her all, this was unsettling. I was no longer the energetic and driven person I had always been. Instead, I had the sensation of fading into the scenery of my own existence.

One morning, while getting ready to go to the diagnostic center, something inside me made me pause. I just couldn't force myself to repeat the routine of another day. Instead, I felt an irresistible pull toward the Ganesh Temple, a location that has consistently provided me with a distinct sense of peace and understanding. This temple occupies a significant spot in my heart—whenever life becomes overwhelming and perplexing or I'm confronted with a tough decision, I tend to go there. It's like the tranquil atmosphere of that location eases my burdens, allowing me to breathe more freely and perceive things with greater clarity.

On that day, I spent several hours sitting silently in the temple, allowing my thoughts to stream as I contemplated my journey. I reflected on the decisions I had taken, the ambitions I had chased, and the obstacles I had encountered. It was a day dedicated to rediscovering myself and achieving a sense of tranquility that eluded me elsewhere. In that silence, I felt anchored, as though the mist had cleared, and everything was coming into view. The temple, enveloped in calming silence and known scenery, provided me the courage to confront whatever challenges awaited.

To me, the Ganesh Temple is more than a site for prayer—it's a refuge where I discover my inner harmony. Regardless of how burdened my heart may be or how unpredictable life appears, entering that temple brings me a sense of calm and strength to continue progressing. That day marked a turning point. As I sat there, I felt both confusion and relief as I realized the truth—I wasn't meant to be in pathology. I had been trying to fit into a role that didn't feel right, and suddenly, I understood why I hadn't felt truly happy. It was as if I had woken up from a dream, seeing my path with newfound clarity.

Throughout my life, I've trusted myself to make my own decisions, especially regarding my education and career. I knew I needed something that would spark joy and excitement in me again, something that would make me feel alive. So, I made a promise to myself to explore other paths to rediscover what truly drives me. It was both terrifying and thrilling, but I knew that, finally, I was ready to take that step forward.

Around that time, the MBA program was very popular, and it felt like a lifeline—a chance to explore something new, to reinvent myself and most importantly, to rebuild the passion I once had. I enrolled in marketing, hoping to move into leadership and management roles. It was an exciting new chapter—one where I could finally align my path with what truly mattered to me. Around this time, a simple incident at home set off an unexpected journey. It was the first day of Diwali, and my tailor refused to deliver the dress I had been waiting for. I was on the couch, feeling quite let down. I gazed at my father and exclaimed, "Baba, I can hardly believe this! I was thrilled to wear that new dress for Diwali, but now the tailor is claiming he can't get it done on time! My father appeared contemplative and responded, "You see, at times, depending on others doesn't necessarily turn out as we wish. Perhaps this is life's method of reminding you that, for the things that genuinely count, you can rely solely on yourself.

I was confused. "But what are you trying to say? I paid in advance and everything!" "It's not about the money," he clarified softly. "It concerns your freedom." When you depend on others to meet your needs, you surrender a portion of control over your own existence. "And when situations don't go as planned, you feel powerless." He then said with a reflective smile, "You've always possessed an incredible sense of fashion. How about considering fashion design as a part-time course?" I paused for a moment, "But Baba, I don't wish to pursue fashion design. "It isn't truly my passion... I merely appreciate it for my own enjoyment."

He smiled kindly, "I'm not suggesting you must create for anyone else. We possess a quality sewing machine at home, and you already have three closets packed with clothes! Why not begin creating and sewing your own dresses instead of relying on others? Consider it a pastime, an activity that you can relish solely for your own pleasure." The more I reflected on it, the more I appreciated the concept. Fashion has always been a passion for me, and among clothing and reading materials, that's where the majority of my funds are spent! It seemed like the ideal answer to my dilemma. So, right after Diwali, I enrolled in a part-time fashion design course, excited to see where this new journey would take me.

How It All Began

When my father announced his plans to renovate our house, I was completely against it. That house held so many memories; I wanted my room to stay exactly as it was, with the same window and the same familiar view. I was never a fan of sleek, modern homes. I loved the warmth of old-fashioned spaces, where every corner had a story to tell. Every little thing in that house—a book, a chair, a table, even our car—felt like part of my life. My parents had chosen each item with me, and I'd been involved in every decision. I'm deeply sentimental about my belongings and can't bring myself to throw anything away. They're part of my journey, filled with memories that I didn't want to lose.

When I flat-out refused the renovation, my father suggested something unexpected. "Why don't you get involved with the renovation?" he said. To ease me into the process, he introduced me to an experienced interior designer, an old friend of his, and asked him to include me in the project. I agreed, seeing it as a chance to learn something new. I think my father wanted me to focus on something fresh, especially since I'd given up my first dream, the medical field, to support our family.

At the same time, I decided to enroll in a fashion design course at the same institute. My curiosity didn't stop there—I also took up interior design, hoping it would help me be part of every detail in our home's transformation. The renovation felt like a way to dive deeper into the design, and soon enough, I found myself genuinely interested in the whole process.

The designer we hired noticed my growing passion and even invited me to sit in on a few client meetings. I had a feeling my father might have encouraged him, knowing I was struggling to find focus after letting go of my original goals. I've always been a very goal-oriented person, and without a clear path, I'd felt a bit lost. Those meetings opened my eyes to a new world, and it was at one of them that I met the person who would become my first boss .... My Guru in Real Estate.

I still remember that meeting vividly. We met at the office of the interior designer, who was working on the interiors of his bungalow and a sample flat for a new project. At the time, I was brand new to this field, still finding my way. The designer, my father's close friend, introduced me as "the daughter of his best friend." It was both comforting and a bit daunting, knowing I was in the company of professionals who had years of experience.

To my surprise, I was given the opportunity to present the initial design for his bungalow. I took a deep breath and began to describe the design in detail as if I'd been part of this field for years. I explained each part of the layout carefully, hoping my passion and excitement would show. That meeting became a pivotal experience for me—a moment where I felt genuinely encouraged and supported.

In that meeting, he saw something beyond just my design ideas; he noticed that I had a natural ability for sales and client interaction. "Why don't you join me?" he asked. At the time, I wasn't sure what path my career would take, but his offer felt like a door opening. So, I took a leap and decided to explore this new opportunity, ready to see where it would lead.

As I decided to enter the real estate industry, I felt excited, but the reactions from my family and friends varied. "Are you absolutely certain about this?" they'd ask, their voices filled with concern. Coming from a family where most were doctors, engineers, or well-educated officials, venturing into real estate felt like stepping into uncharted territory. Real estate wasn't just unfamiliar to them—it seemed unsuitable for women. There were whispers about how builders didn't treat women fairly and how the industry was male-dominated. My family even suggested I open a pathology lab, something they felt was a more "appropriate" choice for a woman. But I wasn't swayed.

The concerns and doubts swirling around me only strengthened my resolve. It wasn't about proving them wrong—it was about following the path that felt right to me. Every time someone questioned my choice, I looked to my role models for strength. Indira Gandhi was someone whose life deeply influenced me, and her journey was a source of immense inspiration for me. Watching her lead with grace in a world not built for her made me realize I could push through my own challenges. She embodied the resilience I needed to face the obstacles in real estate, an industry not always welcoming to women. That inspiration fueled my passion, which hasn't dimmed.

First Steps in Real Estate

I can still recall my first visit to the real estate office in 1998. The energy in the room was undeniable - phones ringing, people bustling about, engaged in discussions about deals and properties. However, I quickly noticed that I was one of just three females in the whole office. It's astonishing, honestly, the level of true support I got from my male coworkers in the initial stages of my career versus what I've faced in later years. At that time, there were individuals who recognized my ongoing learning, and they chose to mentor and guide me. They viewed me not as a rival but as an individual with promise. Some even made extra efforts to guarantee I received the proper training, recognizing that progress stemmed from teamwork and collective knowledge. It was an environment where friendship seemed inherent, and mentorship was promoted.

Still, stepping into the world of real estate felt like entering a foreign land. The jargon—square feet, agreements, bookings—was unfamiliar, and the pace of the industry was relentless. But I've always been quick to adapt. Scanning brochures in minutes, walking through sites, and observing seasoned professionals in action, I found myself drawn in more deeply with each passing day. My boss saw potential in me, and he was right when he told me that real estate was a sector where you could learn endlessly. He didn't just give me a title—he put me through a rigorous two-month training program. I sat with the receptionist, worked with the accounts team, and shadowed the sales team. I learned everything—from the ground up.

Office hours were strict—10 AM to 7 PM, with a lunch break of an hour in between. While everyone left for lunch, I stayed back, eager to absorb more. One day, when the office was empty, a client walked in, curious about a new scheme that had just launched. I sat with him, gave him all the details, and, to my surprise, he booked it on the spot. A few days later, he referred 10 colleagues from his office. That moment felt like a sign— real estate was where I was supposed to be. This wasn't just another job; it was the start of a new journey, and from that point forward, there was no looking back! Real estate wasn't merely about deals or commissions; it was about the lives intertwined with those transactions.

Handing over the keys to a family's new home, I saw their faces transform—lit with joy, filled with tears, laughter, and disbelief. It was in those moments that I realized the weight of what I was doing. I wasn't just selling property; I was delivering on the dreams, hopes, and aspirations people held for their futures. Those moments of shared happiness became my greatest reward. Seeing someone's dream materialize into a tangible, livable space—a sanctuary for their family—was deeply fulfilling. It wasn't just their victory; it felt like mine, too.

What I quickly learned about real estate was that it wasn't just about signing contracts and closing deals. From the outside, it might seem like a straightforward process—find a property, sell it, and move on to the next. But once you're in it, you see that it's so much more. There's a depth to it that I hadn't fully realized until I was in the thick of things. Every client came with their own set of needs, hopes, and concerns. It wasn't just about selling them a space—it was about understanding their vision and their dream for what that space could be. I recall one of my initial interactions with a customer. They talked about their hopes for their new home, imagining the way they would live there. It wasn't just concerning the property; it was also regarding the opportunities it offered. Helping people achieve their goals was very fulfilling and gave me a sense of purpose I didn't anticipate.

Each sale was different, and every conversation was distinct. At times, I would have conversations with individuals who had spent years saving up to purchase their first home. At times, I would encounter individuals seeking to invest in their future. Each transaction was unique, which added to the challenge and excitement of the situation. I had to rapidly master the skills of adjusting, attentively listening, and providing tailored solutions for the individual in front of me. On some occasions, when I gave the possession, the client would invite me for the housewarming ceremony.

It was during this phase of my life, as I grew into my career that I also stepped into a new chapter personally. After my marriage, my name changed from Chaitali to Ketaki—a name chosen with care and thoughtfulness by my father-in-law. The story of how it came to be is one I cherish.

In our family, names hold significance, often carrying with them the weight of tradition and hope for the future. My father-in-law, a man of quiet wisdom, wanted to give me a name that symbolized prosperity and positivity. "Ketaki" is associated with Goddess Laxmi, the goddess of wealth and abundance. He believed the name would serve as a blessing, a reminder of the grace and resilience I brought to our family.

I still remember the moment he announced it. It was simple and understated, yet profound. At first, it felt strange, like wearing a new identity, but over time, I grew into it. The name Ketaki came to symbolize a new beginning—both in my personal life and in my career. It felt like a quiet affirmation.

Following that was the moment that cemented my position in the field—one that came with my initial sale. I can vividly recall being seated at my desk, feeling the anxious excitement of the initial days all around me. A customer entered, and I got the opportunity to chat with him. We discussed his aspirations and his desires for a home, and I became fully engaged in the discussion. Before I realized it, he was prepared to progress, and in an instant, my initial transaction was completed. It was thrilling! A surge of pride and confidence washed over me, confirming my abilities and giving me the reassurance I was seeking.

I was amazed by how fast everything was progressing and how the initial days at work had transformed into something larger than expected. Recognizing that success was not simply a result of luck, I understood that forming connections, empathizing with others, and fulfilling commitments were the key factors that truly mattered.

The Path Becomes Clear

The longer I worked in real estate, the more things began to fit together. It seemed like I belonged in that world, as if the real estate had been patiently anticipating my arrival. Every time I engaged with a customer or made a sale, I felt a newfound sense of meaning. Choosing this wasn't merely a professional decision; rather, it seemed like I had discovered my true purpose. It made me understand that, at times, the routes we take are not the ones we intended, but they are the ones destined for us.

The initial months taught me that real estate involved more than just properties and transactions; it also involved forming connections with individuals and assisting them in achieving their aspirations. And that made me feel extremely satisfied. Witnessing someone move into their new home, knowing you contributed to the process, is truly something unique. I didn't anticipate feeling this, but once it happened, I couldn't ignore it. I discovered the intersection of passion and purpose, which was a significant revelation.

With that clear understanding came a feeling of confidence. I no longer had any doubts about whether real estate was the best choice for me. I was aware of it. Choosing to completely follow through with it no longer required a conscious decision - it was simply a strong intuition within me. I was passionate about real estate, and my mind was prepared to embrace it fully. However, along with that confidence also came the realization that this voyage was still incomplete. If anything, the true difficulties were only starting. What challenges might I encounter as a female in a male-dominated industry? How can I create an environment where I can flourish and develop? I was aware that it would be difficult, but I wasn't afraid. Actually, it spurred me on. The uncertainty should be welcomed, not feared.

This marked the start, and I was prepared to face whatever was to come. Real estate had become more than just a job. It was the place where I felt I fit in perfectly, and I was prepared to fully immerse myself with all of my passion and determination. What was in store for the future? I was unsure. However, one thing I was sure about was that I was fully committed, and the only way was forward!

Rising Above

The Hidden Struggles

From the very beginning, starting out a career in real estate as a woman in a male-dominated industry was a challenge. The sector was not created considering women, as evident from the subtle comments and the more explicit obstacles I encountered. I can recall entering my initial workplace and noticing that I was one of only three females there - me, the receptionist, and the typist. The majority of my coworkers were male, and you could feel the doubt in the air. At each meeting and each project, I felt like there was an implied expectation for me to demonstrate my belonging.

Certainly, I couldn't overlook the emotional impact. Each day, dealing with the prejudices had a negative impact on my mental well-being. It wasn't just about staying on top of the tasks; it was about always needing to demonstrate my worth. There were times when the burden of these expectations seemed too much to bear, but I persisted. Most people were unaware of the pressure, but for me, it felt intimately personal. I constantly felt like I was battling against the expectations of the world.

However, amidst everything, I never allowed outside doubts to influence how I value myself. I was determined not to allow others to dictate my professional identity. Being assertive was crucial—I needed to master the skill of advocating for myself, even in environments where my opinions were not always valued. I was aware that my greatest strength was resilience. Regardless of the obstacles I faced, I always kept in mind my value as a person. I was set on achieving success, and I wasn't going to allow anyone else's opinions to hinder me.

It was challenging, but each little success boosted my self-assurance and established my presence in an industry that wasn't prepared for someone like me.

A Moment of Transformation

There are moments in life that test your spirit, and this was one of those times. I still remember that day when one of my older colleagues in the office had allotted a task to me when I was very new in the field. He wanted me to prepare a cost sheet for a booking. I could not calculate the stamp duty, and he got angry. "Go home and do household work," he said dismissively over a minor mistake I'd made. It was a gut punch. In that instant, I felt like every doubt and bias about women in the workplace was being thrown directly at me. Those words reduced everything I had achieved and aspired to be to a single, outdated notion of what my role as a woman should be. I briefly experienced the pain of those words penetrating deeply. I took the job purely for the experience, not because I needed financial support. If I wanted, I could have easily told my boss and walked away. It was more than just the insult - it symbolized the challenges women encounter and the ongoing need to demonstrate our worth in male-dominated fields.

It wasn't just a setback in my career; it also affected me on an emotional level. Bearing societal pressures can feel like a heavy burden, a silent struggle endured solo. Allowing these types of comments can gradually harm your mental well-being. That night, I recall being unable to sleep, grappling with self-doubt and pondering if those around me had similar thoughts. However, even in that lack of light, there was a small sign of resolve - a message that I had to not allow his words to shape me. What they were unaware of, what he wasn't aware of, was that I was composed of a more resilient substance. I might have allowed that moment to defeat me.

I could have retreated and let his words diminish me. However, I allowed them to serve as my motivation. Whenever self-doubt started to enter my mind, I would tell myself that my value was not based on what others thought. I didn't let someone else's limitations bring me down. That evening, while going over his words in my mind, there was a change within me. I promised myself silently that I wouldn't just exist in this field, I would excel in it.

And, as I mentioned earlier, Trishul became more than just a movie—it became a philosophy. Vijay's resilience in the face of adversity mirrored what I wanted to achieve. I wasn't interested in letting others steer my course. His character showed me that you don't wait for opportunities; you create them. So, rather than letting his words break my confidence, I used them as a tool to sharpen my resolve. But that didn't mean it was easy. There were days when it felt exhausting to carry the weight of these expectations.

Navigating this male-dominated world as a woman often felt like walking a tightrope—one wrong move, and you'd be dismissed as incapable. I had to constantly balance between being assertive enough to be taken seriously without coming off as too aggressive, which could quickly backfire. It was mentally taxing, especially knowing that these battles were often invisible to everyone around me. While men in my position didn't have to think twice about how their actions were perceived, every decision I made was measured twice as hard. Still, I refused to let those challenges shape how I saw myself.

Assertiveness became a tool of survival. I learned that standing up for myself wasn't about being confrontational but about quietly building my confidence and ensuring that others saw my value through my work. I had to prove that I wasn't just capable—I was exceptional. And in a way, the more I was tested, the stronger my resolve became. It wasn't easy, but with every milestone, I learned that the most important opinion of my work was my own. I refused to allow external perceptions to define my identity or potential. That moment with him didn't shatter my confidence—it built it. Every sale, every project, every success from that moment forward was driven by a simple goal: I wasn't going to let anyone tell me what I could or couldn't do. That was my moment of transformation. It wasn't about revenge or proving others wrong. It was about proving to myself that I could rise above any challenge, no matter how personal or painful.

Sometimes, the right mentor steps in just when you need them the most. For me, that person was my first boss, a true mentor, and someone I would come to call my "real estate guru." He wasn't just teaching me the basics of the business—he was shaping how I approached life and work in every sense. I was fresh into the world of real estate, eager but unsure. He saw that spark in me even before I did. His guidance wasn't just technical—it was about attitude, work ethic, and approach.

Early on, I remember asking him for leave when I had personal commitments, was newly married, and was trying to balance my life. His response was clear and straightforward, something I've carried with me throughout my career. He said, "If you want to reach the top and earn a salary equal to your male counterparts, you must be passionate, hard-working, and avoid making excuses." That advice stayed with me. He didn't hand out advice for the sake of it—he lived it and expected the same from everyone around him, including me.

He never made me feel less capable because I was a woman in a male-dominated industry. Gender wasn't the focus; effort and results were. In a time when gender bias was the norm, he stood out. It wasn't that he had to give me any special encouragement—he expected me to perform at the same level as anyone else. It was empowering in a way that wasn't loud or dramatic but consistent and steady. Through him, I learned everything that truly mattered in real estate. From building client relationships to mastering agreements and sales tactics, no detail was too small, and no task was too menial.

I shadowed him in every corner of the business, absorbing not just what he said but how he worked. He never allowed me to settle for mediocrity. He never permitted me to accept average quality. "Work Hard" was not merely words for him; it was a lifestyle that deeply resonated with me. He had a mix of serene control and unwavering commitment in his personality. He didn't hurry through tasks, nor did he support shortcuts. His work ethic established the atmosphere in the office—concentrated, resolute, and consistently involved.

I realized that leadership was not just about major decisions but also about setting an example in every small detail. Under his guidance, I acquired the ability to handle difficult situations with composure and resolve. He possessed a calm wisdom, never yelling commands but consistently ensuring your growth and learning. It was a critical time in my early career as it provided me with the resources necessary not only to survive in the real estate industry but also to excel. These early lessons became the foundation of everything that followed. His advice shaped how I approached challenges, how I pushed through tough moments, and how I never allowed myself to fall back on excuses. It was never just about real estate; it was about the bigger picture—being resilient, passionate, and ready for whatever came next.

Pushing Through

As I settled into my role, I was truly immersed in the work. Each day presented a fresh challenge, yet I remained dedicated to continuous learning and pushing my limits. The guidance and advice from my mentor always stayed with me, encouraging me to persevere. Suddenly, life presented me with a surprising twist: I was expecting twins. The thrill was genuine, yet the daunting task of juggling pregnancy with a busy career was also very real. The doctors advised me to take a break, highlighting the intricacies, but I couldn't fathom pausing at that moment.

I had poured my heart into building my career, and I wasn't about to let anything slow me down—not yet. I knew a break was inevitable, but I was determined to leave on my own terms, with everything in place. Real estate had become more than a job to me; it was a passion that fueled my days. I thrived on the challenges, the fast pace, and the thrill of closing deals. For the first time, I felt truly connected to my work, and I wasn't ready to step away from it.

Even during my pregnancy, I kept pushing forward. There were days I would visit the hospital for treatments, get a saline drip, and head straight back to the office, ready to tackle the next task. I chose a hospital just ten minutes away, making it easier to transition seamlessly between appointments and work. It wasn't easy—balancing the physical demands of pregnancy with the relentless pace of real estate—but I was driven. The energy I found in my work seemed to outweigh the exhaustion, and I felt deeply committed to every project I touched.

The demands were constant, but so was my sense of purpose. I wasn't just keeping up; I was fully engaged, excited even, to be at the center of it all. There were moments when people questioned how I managed it, but I never doubted myself. I remember thinking, *"I've come this far; I can handle this too."* And I did.

I worked diligently until shortly before my children were born. Looking back, it was an incredibly busy and challenging time—balancing pregnancy and the intensity of my work—but I wouldn't have done it any other way. Leaving when I did wasn't about pushing limits or proving a point; it was about making sure I left on a note of fulfillment and responsibility, ensuring the work I cared about so deeply was uninterrupted. It was exhausting, yes, but also deeply rewarding—a testament to how much this career had become a part of me.

What motivated me in the last weeks wasn't just the desire to complete the task but also the sense of purpose I discovered in the real estate industry. I had a strong bond with the task at hand, and moving away felt like abandoning a piece of myself. I aimed to demonstrate to myself that I could continue advancing despite facing obstacles.

However, it was certainly challenging. There were times when I was tired and wondered how much longer I could maintain the same level of energy. However, there was a part of me that continued to urge me to consider the larger perspective. This wasn't just about work - it was about establishing my presence in a challenging industry. I had a goal, and there was nothing that could prevent me from reaching it. This vision motivated me, even on the most challenging days.

As I look back on those days, pushing through every obstacle felt like a constant balancing act. From carving a space in real estate to managing the challenges of becoming a mother, I was building a foundation not just for my career but for the life I envisioned. But even as things began to settle, life has its own plans, doesn't it? Little did I know the next chapter would take me on a new, unexpected journey. The real challenges were only just beginning.

Stepping Back In

A Fresh Start

After five months of maternity leave, I felt a strong urge to return to work. Balancing the responsibilities of being a new mother with my professional aspirations was daunting, but I was determined to stay true to my goals. My passion for real estate had become a driving force in my life. However, my decision to rejoin the real estate industry was met with resistance from my family. They believed I should focus on starting my own business—anything but real estate. Despite their objections, I was resolute in my choice.

My first boss had played a pivotal role in shaping my career. Under his guidance, I gained a thorough understanding of the real estate sector, which ignited a deep passion within me. This passion only grew stronger over time. I knew that to excel, I had to stay informed. Even while managing the demands of motherhood and caring for my sons, I made it a point to read the newspaper daily to keep up with market trends.

Back then, social media did not exist, and newspapers were the primary source of information and advertising for developers. Saturdays were particularly significant, as they featured real estate advertisements and insights that helped me understand the market dynamics. It became a ritual for me to immerse myself in these pages, equipping myself with knowledge and strategies to navigate the industry.

Returning to real estate was more than just a career decision—it was a statement of my commitment to my passion and my belief in my ability to balance motherhood and a challenging profession. Looking back, those moments of persistence laid the foundation for the many milestones I would achieve in the years to come.

Transitioning back to work after six months with my newborns was a bittersweet challenge. Those early days with them were transformative—my whole world had shifted in ways I couldn't have predicted. Each coo, each tiny smile, filled me with awe but also with a new layer of responsibility. Late nights and early mornings blended together in a blur of feeding, rocking, and soft lullabies. For someone used to the rush of real estate, being home with two little ones was both rewarding and humbling, grounding me in ways I'd never imagined. But as the months passed, the drive to return to work surfaced again. The idea of getting back wasn't just about a job anymore; it was about building a life that balanced my personal dreams with my new role as a mother. I wanted to create something meaningful, something my kids could one day look at with pride.

Finding a job then wasn't like it is now. Online job portals didn't exist yet, so I relied on the Tuesday *Sakal* and Wednesday *Times of India* job listings. After combing through each page, circling listings and making calls, I finally found a role that aligned perfectly with my interests. Back then, the concept of separate Sales and CRM (Customer Relationship Management) departments did not exist. Both functions were integrated into a single team, requiring professionals to handle not only the sales process but also the post-sales customer engagement. This dual responsibility demanded a diverse skill set—closing deals, managing customer expectations, resolving issues, and ensuring satisfaction—all under one umbrella.

This structure, though challenging, allowed me to gain a 360-degree perspective on the customer journey, from the initial interaction to the after-sales service. It taught me the importance of building strong relationships with clients, anticipating their needs, and addressing concerns proactively. This hands-on experience proved to be invaluable, as it gave me a holistic understanding of the business, shaping my expertise in both sales strategy and customer relationship management.

Even amidst these responsibilities, I remained committed to learning. Reading the newspaper daily and analyzing real estate trends became my way of staying ahead in an industry that was just beginning to evolve. Those early days, with their combined roles and challenges, were instrumental in shaping the professional I am today. They prepared me to adapt to change, juggle multiple responsibilities, and find innovative solutions—skills that continue to serve me well in my career.

Walking into that office for the first time, I felt the shift. I realized how different it was from my previous job. It felt like stepping into a new world and adapting to an unfamiliar culture. Here, my superiors were addressed by their initials instead of the familiar "Bhabhi" I'd used for my former boss's wife. The formality, the structure—everything required a certain finesse.

I shifted from my usual Indian formals to Western attire and found myself quickly learning the nuances of corporate life. I switched my mode of communication from a pager that I'd used during my initial years to a mobile phone that was gifted to me by my father during my first job. Even with calls being costly, having that mobile felt like a rite of passage, a step into a new professional era. Taking on both CRM and sales introduced a level of commitment I hadn't encountered before, and I felt my resolve deepen. The twin challenges of motherhood and a career in real estate added layers to my responsibilities, but it was the right kind of challenge. I was determined not only to find balance but to excel in each role.

Growth, Validation, and Personal Trials

Returning to work, I stepped into a new chapter that demanded more of me than ever before. This phase was marked by a shift in both the responsibilities I carried and the company I kept. I was no longer the eager executive just trying to find her place—I was working with seasoned brokers, handling projects that boasted impressive amenities and elevated standards. Real estate had evolved from a job into a challenge I was prepared to tackle head-on. Each interaction felt like a new lesson, each project a new milestone, and I was determined to prove my capability, not just to others, but to myself.

Balancing both sales and CRM without the clear divisions common today adds complexity. From booking appointments at the head office to handling loan proposals and facilitating the transfer of possession, I was managing every step of the client journey. This responsibility brought out a resolve in me I hadn't fully tapped into before. The hard work didn't go unnoticed, either; within two years, I found myself promoted, with the task of leading a team for the first time. It was an enormous shift, one that felt like a validation of all the challenges I'd faced up to that point.

Then came a moment that felt almost poetic in its timing, a moment that really validated my journey. I had the chance to interview a former critic from my very first job. This was the same person who had, in those early days, dismissed my capabilities, belittled my potential and made me feel insulted. I couldn't forget that moment; it had hit hard back then. But here I was now, sitting across the table from him, interviewing him for a position below me. Life has an uncanny way of proving that hard work, if consistent, paves the way forward. I kept my professionalism intact, but inside, I was filled with quiet pride, knowing how much I'd grown. It wasn't about proving anyone wrong—it was a moment where I proved to myself that perseverance matters and that it carries you forward when you least expect it.

However, life wasn't without its trials. During this period, I lost two of the most important pillars in my life—my grandmother and my father. Their loss was immense. My grandmother, who had given me my name and instilled resilience in me, and my father, who had always been my pillar of support, were no longer there to lean on. My father's sudden passing made me feel like I'd lost the very foundational element of my life, and navigating those times felt very daunting. It was an ordinary day; he was going to his factory, and then, in a moment, everything changed. An unexpected heart failure took him away from us. But even in that corporate environment, my boss supported me through it. That sense of empathy reminded me of what true leadership looks like, and it encouraged me to be resilient despite the grief I was carrying.

There were moments that lightened the weight of all the responsibilities and even the losses. I'll always remember the little joys, like when our MD and CEO would step out to join us in watching cricket on the common TV—those moments gave our team a sense of unity. And then, there was a day I'll never forget. The Managing Director (MD) of the office was a highly experienced professional, especially in land acquisition. He shared invaluable lessons with me, much like my father once did, emphasizing the importance of self-reliance. He often said, *"Even as a leader, you must stay grounded and actively involved to stay informed about what's happening around you."*

At that time, land acquisition processes heavily relied on meticulous documentation. Scanners were not yet in use; only Xerox and fax machines were available. I vividly remember how, despite his seniority, he would personally operate the Xerox machine in his spacious cabin if no assistance was available. This humility and hands-on approach kept him grounded and contributed significantly to the company's rise to the number one position.

Ever since my first job, I'd noticed a pattern: my bosses always seemed to assign me tasks beyond my role. Why me? I'd wonder at times, but over time, I began to realize they saw potential. So, when my boss asked me to accompany our Business Head to meet a well-known real estate agent, I didn't question it. During that time, everyone in the organization was a multitasker, wearing multiple hats to ensure the work got done. There were no distinct or specialized departments as we see in structured organizations today. Instead, the entire operation relied on a close-knit team of just 4-5 key individuals who managed everything. Each person had to be versatile, taking on a variety of responsibilities and stepping into different roles as needed. This lean setup fostered a strong sense of collaboration and adaptability, as every team member contributed to multiple facets of the business. It was a challenging yet rewarding environment that honed skills, built resilience, and emphasized the importance of teamwork. I respected everyone's roles and figured my boss asked me to tag along just to observe how our Business Head went about his job. This agent handled investments for celebrities and had set up meetings with a famous cricketer and a Bollywood actor. After meeting the cricketer, the Business Head casually mentioned we'd make a quick stop to meet a Bollywood actor before lunch. What I didn't know was that the entire office had planned a surprise for me! They all knew of my lifelong admiration for Amitabh Bachchan, fondly known as "Big B." Every year, I'd celebrated his birthday on October 11th—something I'd been doing since I was young. This wasn't just a regular work meeting; it was a gift from my colleague, a gesture that made me realize the kindness of the few incredible colleagues I'd been lucky to meet. As we entered the office, the agent turned to me with a smile and said, "Ma'am, you have only five minutes. Let's go inside." Five minutes! My heart was racing; goosebumps prickled all over my skin. Could this really be happening? I was trying hard just to keep my breath steady when Amitji's PA came out to let us know he'd be there shortly. When he walked in, it was magical. His presence filled the room, and I couldn't believe I was standing there.

The agent introduced me as one of Big B's biggest fans, and he greeted me warmly: "Ketakiji, kaisi hain aap?" I was speechless, completely in awe! Somehow, I managed to tell him how I'd seen all his movies, including his lesser-known ones like *Saudagar* and *Saat Hindustani.* He smiled and, with that gracious warmth, thanked me, saying, "Hum aapka dhanyawad karna chahte hain." Those few minutes felt timeless—I remember each second, his iconic black hair and white beard and his gentle manner. It was a dream come true. Afterward, I couldn't thank my colleague and the agent enough. I walked out of there, overwhelmed by gratitude and emotion, barely able to hold back tears. The next day, everyone at the office was waiting to hear every detail, knowing how much Big B and his movies meant to me. Some of his films I've seen two or three times, and each one still feels fresh. Meeting him was more than an encounter—it's a memory I'll cherish forever.

A Pivotal Moment: Discovering Law

An opportunity arrived out of nowhere, but it marked a turning point I'll never forget. One afternoon, while reviewing a project file during a meeting with a banker, I noticed something off in the development agreement. It was a subtle but significant error in the legal phrasing—a detail that could easily have slipped by. I paused, thinking about my training under my first boss and how he'd always encouraged me to be thorough, to not settle until I'd combed through every detail. It felt natural to follow that advice, so I flagged the error and informed the bank representative that I'd need time to revisit the file. I immediately brought the issue to my MD's attention.

What happened next was unexpected: surprised by my observation, he quickly arranged a meeting with the chairman, believing it warranted his attention. This wasn't the kind of meeting you'd expect for someone in my position! I felt a mix of nerves and excitement as I walked into that room. The chairman, a highly respected figure, asked me several questions about the agreement, the legal documentation, and what I'd noticed. I explained everything as best I could, calling on all the knowledge I'd gained from my early training. He listened closely, and by the end of our discussion, he nodded approvingly. That moment of recognition, seeing that he valued what I brought to the table—it was something that made me feel truly seen in a way I hadn't felt before.

As I got up to leave, he stopped me and said something that would change my career's course. "You should consider studying law," he suggested. He went on to say how my knowledge of legal documentation could add even greater depth to my work in real estate. His words resonated deeply with me, and I couldn't shake them off. The thought of expanding my skills in such a powerful direction was both thrilling and intimidating. I was already balancing so much, but the chance to step into legal studies felt like a door I didn't want to close. It was a decision that felt right.

However, discussing this decision with my family brought its own set of challenges. My mother was hesitant, her voice laced with concern. "If you're not wearing a white coat, you can't wear a black one," she said, referencing her worry about me entering the legal field. And my father-in-law, who had had a negative experience with lawyers, was opposed to the idea altogether. Their hesitation weighed on me. I wanted them to see that this wasn't about a shift in the profession but a way to deepen my understanding and expertise in the field I was committed to. So, I promised them that I wouldn't apply for a license—I was in this for knowledge alone. I knew how important their support was to me, and I wanted them to feel comfortable with this next step.

With my family's cautious blessing, I enrolled in a top law school within two months. My boss's generosity during this period was something I'll never forget. He allowed me flexible hours to balance both work and studies without deducting my salary. His belief in me was invaluable, a reminder of the impact true leadership can have on one's journey. The next three years were intense, juggling my responsibilities at work and my commitments to my law classes. It was a challenging period, no doubt, but it also turned out to be one of the most rewarding phases of my life.

Within two months, I was admitted to a top law school, where attendance was mandatory, and the first lecture was at 7 AM sharp. Those early days brought a rush of excitement but also a tinge of doubt. Could I really juggle both? I was already handling CRM and sales, though the office timings were flexible, and here I was, about to dive headfirst into legal studies! It wasn't just another course; it was a commitment. I knew balancing everything would be intense, and yet, the idea of it sparked a fire in me. Thankfully, my boss, understanding the importance of this journey, generously allowed me flexible office hours. I never asked for special treatment, but sometimes, opportunities find you just when you need them most.

During my law school days, whenever I had holidays, I would spend them working full-time at the office. I ensured I utilized my time effectively, taking leaves only during exams to focus on my studies. Those formative years under the guidance of my boss played a pivotal role in shaping my legal acumen. His mentorship was instrumental in building the foundation of my expertise in legal drafting. Even today, I make it a point to visit him as a token of gratitude for his invaluable support and encouragement whenever I achieve something significant.

Thanks to his training and my dedication, I can now draft even the most critical documents in minutes, structuring and articulating them with precision and clarity. My law college professor often praised me for this skill,

When I reflect on the first 15 years of my career, I realize I achieved everything without demanding it. My hard work and commitment were always recognized by my bosses and colleagues, who continue to appreciate my efforts even today. I often reconnect with them to share my milestones, and their admiration motivates me to aim higher.

One thing I deeply admired about my boss was his belief that when employees grow, the company grows automatically. This forward-thinking philosophy created an environment of mutual respect, long term relationship and empowerment. In today's world, where many prioritize the company's growth over individual development, his approach remains a rare and cherished perspective that shaped my professional values.

There's something empowering about having leaders who genuinely recognize your potential. With that support, I pushed through, day by day, class by class, navigating the demands of law school, my responsibilities at work and my role as a mother. It was challenging—some days felt endless—but I was finally making real strides toward a vision I had kept close to my heart.

After completing my law degree, the pieces started falling into place. I took on a major role, managing the land acquisition for a large township. This wasn't just a milestone in my career; it was a moment of true validation. Years of study, countless hours of hard work, and the constant balancing act—it was all paying off. Each project, each negotiation, and every piece of land secured became more than just tasks. They were stepping stones, proof of growth, and moments of pride. I was still handling CRM, managing client relationships and the sales pipeline, yet I felt I was expanding in every way, handling multiple roles that challenged me and stretched my skills. This chapter of my journey reaffirmed something essential: with each challenge I faced, I was building the strength to meet whatever lay ahead. It was more than just a job—it was proof of how far I had come, and it fueled my confidence for the future.

When Life Takes a Turn

A Sudden Halt

I still recall those days at my first corporate job. It was there that I truly began to grow—not just in experience but in learning to lead a team and guide others. Watching my team progress was deeply rewarding, and the experience brought lasting connections. Many of those I trained still reach out on Guru Purnima, a tradition that fills me with pride each year. Yet, as rewarding as it was, destiny had other plans. Looking back, I realize that my grandmother's instinct to help others—something I've always been grateful for—is what led me to that fateful day. Sometimes, it's those unplanned twists of fate that carry the weight of both blessings and unforeseen trials.

It was on an ordinary day that everything changed…

That day felt like any other, but it would soon unravel into something far from ordinary. One of my team members, someone I'd mentored and grown close to, had confided in me earlier about a painful issue. His elder brother had cheated him out of a property—a place he had every right to own. I took it upon myself to help him navigate the process of transferring the property back to his name. It was a complex effort, yet seeing his relief made every step worth it. Soon after, he began building a small house on that land, and when it was finally complete, he invited me to the housewarming. That morning, looking at the cloudy sky, I called him to say I might not make it, given the weather and distance. His wife took the phone, her voice thick with emotion, almost pleading for me to join them, even if only for a brief time. She mentioned they'd planned everything, and my absence would leave a void in their celebration.

It was also Mangalagaur, and I had plans to attend a pooja close to home. But the earnestness in her voice tugged at me. So, in my saree, with half-day leave arranged, I set out with a sense of purpose, thinking it would be a quick visit. There was no Google Maps then, so I took a female colleague along to help with directions, knowing the road might be tricky. The journey stretched longer than expected as we stopped frequently, asking locals for guidance. The house was further out than I'd anticipated, nearly two and a half hours away in a remote area. Finally, we parked at the base of a small hill and began the climb. The road up was unpaved, littered with loose stones, and I slowed my steps, balancing my saree as we walked.

Then came the moment that would change everything. I saw a truck coming down the slope, speeding and swerving as if the driver had lost control. My colleague was ahead, but I was cautious, my movements restrained by my saree. Before I could even react, the wind caught my pallu, and it tangled on a hook at the back of the truck. In that instant, I felt a sudden, terrifying tug pulling me along with it. I tried to regain my footing, but my balance gave way, and I was dragged. Somehow, I managed to free my saree, but not without injury. My face was cut, my knee was scraped and bleeding, and worst of all, my tongue had been injured and cut —I couldn't even form words. Pain was radiating through my entire body, but I was numb with shock. My colleague, alarmed and unable to drive, called another colleague who was attending the same ceremony that I was planning to attend. By the time help arrived, my saree was torn, my face was bruised, and I was struggling to keep myself upright. They helped rush me to a nearby hospital, where the initial treatment began.

The facilities were limited, and seeing my injuries, my family arranged my transfer to a larger hospital. Once there, doctors confirmed the extent of the damage—fractures in my nose, knee, neck, and elbow. I had to stay under observation, my face so bruised it was unrecognizable. For the next week, I was confined to the hospital, grappling with pain and the realization that recovery would be far from simple. The doctor insisted on bed rest for a minimum of three months, cautioning me that anything less would delay my healing. The physical wounds, though severe, were easier to accept than the overwhelming sense of helplessness. As I lay in that hospital bed, the full impact of what had happened washed over me. Recovery would be long, not just for my body but for my mind.

The days following the accident were far harder than I had ever anticipated. As someone who thrived on the action, strategy, and seeing projects come to life, being confined to my home felt like a cruel twist of fate. It wasn't just the physical pain—it was the emotional toll of being cut off from the work I loved, the work that defined me.

A deep sense of incompleteness gnawed at me as I watched my meticulously crafted plans unravel. Those ambitious projects I had poured my heart into—the land acquisitions, the bold new initiatives— suddenly felt like distant dreams slipping through my fingers. I had always been a planner, someone who thought ten steps ahead. Yet here I was, facing a reality where control seemed impossible.

For three years, I managed to balance flexible hours while pursuing my law studies and preparing for exams. It was a testament to my dedication and belief that with enough willpower, I could achieve anything. And I had big dreams—I wanted to expand my role to lead two departments. I envisioned myself steering the ship, driving decisions, and breaking new ground.

But the accident changed everything. The physical limitations were only part of the story. It was the enforced pause, the realization that I could no longer chase my ambitions in the same way, that hit me the hardest. After much reflection, I had to make the painful decision to step down, knowing that it wasn't just a job I was walking away from—it was a part of my identity.

The experience was humbling and transformative. It forced me to reevaluate my priorities and discover resilience in ways I hadn't before. Though the journey was challenging, it also became a pivotal moment of growth, shaping my understanding of leadership, adaptability, and the importance of embracing change.

I remember holding my resignation letter with a hollow ache, feeling that leaving was the only way to avoid hindering the team's progress. But my boss saw something in me, even when I struggled to see it myself. He urged me to stay on part-time. Reluctantly, I agreed, finding relief in those hours, knowing I was still contributing. After three months of bed rest, I started working part-time. The journey to the office took a toll on me physically and emotionally. With no Uber or Ola back then and unable to drive due to my back injury, I'd make that hour-long commute by auto-rickshaw, bracing myself for the day ahead. I would pour all I had into my work, determined to stay connected to what I loved doing.

Even though I needed only around 5 hours every day to finish all my tasks, challenges arose. Some colleagues began to resent my shortened hours and, over time, made it clear through small, bitter actions. They believed I was getting special treatment, and the undercurrents of hostility were hard to ignore, adding to the emotional weight of my recovery. My body needed rest, but so did my spirit, weary from fighting battles on all fronts. After two months of trying to balance everything, I faced the reality I'd tried so hard to avoid: my health had to come first. The constant physical toll, the tension in the office—it was all too much. I knew I had to let go. With a heavy heart, I approached my boss once more. Though he was reluctant, he could see the toll it was taking on me, and he finally agreed to let me go. As I left, it felt like I was leaving a part of myself.

<u>Healing Inside and Out</u>

After I resigned, the journey to recovery became a central part of my life—physically demanding and mentally draining, yet incredibly transformative. Every morning, I faced a new set of challenges, from struggling to regain my physical strength to finding the willpower to push forward. It was during this time that I realized healing wasn't going to be a straightforward path but a long battle with setbacks and moments of doubt. There were days I questioned if I'd ever fully recover, but gradually, I began to accept that this wasn't just a physical process; it was about building resilience, mentally and emotionally. The accident had left me with a profound sense of loss, almost as though a part of my identity had been put on hold. Real estate, which had been a pillar in my life, was now a distant memory as I focused on simply making it through each day. I missed the purpose my work gave me, and with every step toward physical recovery, I felt a renewed determination to grow in other ways, too. If I couldn't dive back into my career just yet, I could at least make use of this time to learn and broaden my skills.

During this time, as I was fully immersed in my recovery process, my family stepped in out of worry for my health and the impact the accident had on me. They had always been concerned about the dangers of my career in real estate. So, they took me to a renowned astro-numerologist, a figure known for his insights and predictions. Though I was skeptical, I went along, understanding their intentions. He studied my chart closely, and then, looking up, he declared, "Your number is '1.' This is the number of the Sun that always shines. You're meant to lead, to be in business rather than a traditional job." It was almost surreal when he mentioned famous business tycoons while talking about the potential he saw in me. It felt both strange and oddly validating, as if fate was gently nudging me in a direction I hadn't fully considered. His belief in me was unwavering, and he even suggested that I change the spelling of my name from "Ketaki" to "Kettaki" to align with numerological principles. At the time, I didn't act on his advice—partly because of my own hesitation and largely due to family pressure. The idea seemed too unconventional, and I didn't feel ready to embrace it.

My family, inspired by his words, began to encourage me to think of alternatives. They suggested that maybe, for the time being, I step back from the intense demands of real estate and consider a business that would allow me flexibility—a space where I could focus on my health and be close to my young children. My background in fashion design, an avenue I had once dabbled in but never pursued as a career, suddenly emerged as a possible path forward. It had always been a passion of mine—a creative outlet that allowed me to express myself in vibrant and unique ways. Everyone admired my impeccable dressing sense and a keen eye for fashion. It wasn't just about wearing clothes—it was about making a statement, reflecting my personality, and carrying myself with confidence. My taste in fashion often became a topic of appreciation among friends, colleagues, and even acquaintances.

Over the years, my love for style translated into a collection that I took great pride in. My bedroom held not one but three to four wardrobes, each brimming with dresses, outfits, sarees and fabrics I had carefully curated. Each piece had a story—some were purchased during travels, some were gifted, and many were chosen for their unique appeal or cultural significance. People often teased me about my love for fashion, playfully asking if I was secretly running a boutique from my bedroom. Little did they know, the thought of making it more than a passion had crossed my mind. I had an innate sense for color, texture, and style—a skill I honed through years of experimenting with patterns and fabrics, both for myself and for others.

Fashion, for me, has always been more than material—it's a form of self-expression. Whether attending a meeting, hosting an event, or simply stepping out for a casual gathering, I ensured that my attire resonated with the occasion and my mood. It wasn't about following trends; it was about defining my own style, which became an extension of who I am.

This flair for dressing not only boosted my confidence but also became an integral part of my identity, leaving a lasting impression on those around me.

The idea of revisiting fashion design felt both exciting and daunting. Could this be a new chapter in my journey, one where I combine creativity with entrepreneurship? It was a field where I could thrive, leveraging my sense of aesthetics and the joy I found in helping others feel confident through what they wore. The thought sparked something within me—a sense of possibility, a belief that every ending is just the beginning of something new.

This realization marked the start of yet another layer to my story—proof that life's detours often lead to unexpected and beautiful destinations. With my family's encouragement, I took a leap and opened a boutique, pouring my energy into creating a space that reflected my sense of style and vision. Within two months, it became profitable, a development that brought a sense of accomplishment I hadn't felt in a long time. The boutique wasn't just a business—it was proof that, even through setbacks, growth and success were within reach.

As I continued to regain my health, I found myself not only healing but also evolving. The accident forced me to step back and reconsider my journey, opening my mind to new possibilities and reinforcing a belief in my own resilience. Although I still felt the pull of real estate, I knew that this time—this chapter—was meant for healing, learning, and building a foundation that would carry me forward. It wasn't long after I'd begun to feel a renewed sense of purpose at my boutique that real estate found me again. One day, a relative from a small town in Maharashtra visited and mentioned that her husband, a businessman eager to explore real estate, needed advice on land acquisition, documentation and design. She asked if I could help, and though I hadn't been planning on reentering the field, there was a tug—a familiar feeling that perhaps I wasn't quite done with real estate.

We arranged a meeting, and as we discussed land acquisition strategies and project design, the process in Pune and many more topics, something clicked. It felt as if I was reigniting a part of myself that had been resting but not forgotten. We set up a plan where I'd work with him for a couple of hours each day, either at his office or from my boutique, which was just a short walk away. What began as two hours turned into three, sometimes four. Real estate was slowly taking root in my daily routine again, but this time with the flexibility I needed for my health and family. Soon, I was actively helping him with land acquisitions in Pune and Navi Mumbai. He had launched his first residential project in Pune, and I was very happy because I had helped him with it from the initial stage. He asked me to join his office in a very senior role, but I refused because I always feel that joining a family friend's or relative's business is not a good idea. It often spoils the relationship. Real estate was slowly finding its way back into my daily routine, but this time with a renewed sense of balance. I approached it differently, prioritizing flexibility to accommodate both my health and my family. The pace was more measured, yet the passion remained as strong as ever.

With this, my passion was back, and I was filled with fresh energy. I hadn't realized how much I'd missed the thrill of negotiating, the satisfaction of seeing projects take shape, and the sense of accomplishment that real estate brought me. Each project, every land deal, felt like a piece of my own journey back to what I loved.

When family members learned that I was once again involved with real estate, there was resistance. They worried about me and about the intensity of the industry. I managed to reassure them, insisting that my focus remained on the boutique while I consulted on a few projects here and there. And it was true—the boutique was still thriving. Due to my customer-friendly nature, I got repeat clients in the boutique, and it was much more profitable than expected. I had a good set of staff that managed everything, even during my absences. Yet, real estate felt like destiny was calling, something that was as much a part of me as ever.

Embracing New Challenges

While I was successfully balancing my boutique and minor real estate consultations, an unexpected opportunity presented itself. An old friend, now a zonal head for a top real estate developer, reached out, offering me a chance to lead three land-plotting projects. This wasn't just any offer—it was an invitation to expand my real estate expertise in new directions. The excitement was undeniable, but it came with a decision I hadn't anticipated: should I sell the boutique that had become my anchor? The more I thought about it, the more conflicted I felt. On one hand, I cherished the boutique and the creative freedom it offered. On the other, the plotting projects stirred a passion I'd never quite shaken. My heart felt torn with all the deliberation, so one day, feeling overwhelmed, I went back to the Ganesh temple, hoping for clarity. Standing before the deity, I found myself filled with a sense of purpose—real estate was where I belonged. This decision was mine to make. With that conviction, I returned home and, instead of asking for approval, outright informed my family of my plan. Naturally, they were upset and worried about my health and well-being. I was not yet allowed to drive, and they worried about my commute to and from work. They tried to dissuade me, but the call of real estate was too strong to ignore, and so, with a heavy heart but firm resolve, I sold the boutique "as-is" and joined my friend in this new venture. Even though it was a senior role, many, including my family, considered it foolish when I decided to leave my highly profitable boutique business and rejoin the real estate industry as an employee. My boutique was thriving—I had the flexibility and freedom I always valued, financial stability, and a reliable team that ensured smooth operations even in my absence. It was a venture that many would consider the pinnacle of success and fulfillment.

Despite this, I chose to return to real estate—a field that had always felt like a part of my identity. The decision wasn't easy. Leaving behind the autonomy and comfort of running my own business to step into the structured environment of an organization was a significant shift. My family, who had seen the success I built, questioned why I would give it up to re-enter a challenging and unpredictable industry.

For me, however, real estate was more than a profession—it was my calling. The chance to lead at a senior level and contribute to an industry I deeply believed in outweighed the skepticism and doubts. While I understood their concerns, I knew this was a step closer to my true purpose and a reflection of my unwavering passion for the sector. Fashion is my hobby, which is limited to myself, but real estate is my passion.

In hindsight, what appeared to be a risky choice to others was, for me, a reaffirmation of my commitment to my values and dreams.

Leading these plotting projects was a thrilling experience. My background in land acquisition, legal aspects, and residential sales gave me the tools I needed, but plotting was a new frontier. Each project brought fresh challenges, but with a supportive team and a renewed sense of purpose, I succeeded in selling the plots faster than I'd expected. After successfully selling the plotting projects, I gained immense confidence in my ability to sell, strategize, and execute effectively within the real estate sector. The achievement validated my belief that I could take on any challenge in real estate and deliver exceptional results. While the initial commitment was to focus on selling three plotting projects, this success inspired me to look beyond.

I realized that my true potential lay not just in sales but in leveraging the comprehensive knowledge I had accumulated over the years. From understanding market trends and planning projects to executing strategies and navigating complexities, I developed a 360-degree perspective of the industry. This prompted me to step back and reassess my professional goals.

Rather than continuing in a narrowly defined role, I decided to seek a profile that would allow me to apply my entire skill set while also expanding my expertise in real estate. I was eager to embrace opportunities where I could grow, contribute strategically, and gain deeper insights into the industry's multifaceted aspects. This decision marked a pivotal point in my career as I transitioned from focusing on short-term achievements to pursuing a broader vision of excellence and leadership in real estate.

Not long after the success with the land plotting projects, another opportunity surfaced that felt like a natural next step in my career. A prominent developer's sales department offered me a role as Head of Business Development. It felt like the perfect fit, aligning with my skills in sales, management, and, of course, real estate. For the first time in a while, I felt like the pieces were falling into place—I was ready to dive in and make a significant impact. However, as I settled into the role, it became clear that the work environment was far from supportive. The excitement I'd initially felt started to wear thin as the atmosphere grew tense, even toxic. Team morale was low, collaboration was strained, and any sense of enthusiasm quickly fizzled out. For someone who thrived on a positive, driven work culture, this was a challenging situation. Though the MD was supportive and encouraging, my colleagues held a very different mindset. Their intentions and attitudes made it clear that they believed women had no place in the core aspects of real estate. In their view, only men were capable of driving the industry forward, and any woman entering the field was relegated to limited roles such as junior-level sales, receptionist, or accountant.

This narrow and biased perception was not just disheartening—it was infuriating. For someone like me, who had already demonstrated the ability to sell, strategize, and execute successfully, being judged solely on my gender rather than my capabilities was unacceptable. This was my first bad experience in the real estate industry, and it left a lasting impression.

The culture was deeply toxic, dominated by rigid hierarchies and resistance to change. Navigating such an environment was challenging, as I was constantly battling not just for recognition of my work but also for the right to be treated as an equal. It was a stark reminder of the biases that persist in traditionally male-dominated industries.

Despite this, I refused to let their negativity define my journey. Instead, this experience strengthened my resolve to challenge such stereotypes and prove that women are just as capable—if not more so—of excelling in real estate and leading it with vision and expertise.

However, my selfless commitment to the role was not enough to fight the pressure that was weighing me down with every passing day. After six months, I had to face a difficult decision. Leaving this position felt like I was stepping away from an incredible opportunity, but the work culture was making it impossible to grow and thrive. In the end, I realized that a title and position mean little if the environment doesn't support your well-being or growth. Leaving wasn't easy, but it taught me a vital lesson: success isn't just about the job title or the responsibilities—it's about the kind of place that genuinely lets you flourish.

When one door closes, another opens—or, sometimes, we have to create our own path. As I looked ahead, I knew I couldn't wait around for the perfect chance to arrive. Equipped with new skills, hard-won resilience, and a resolve to keep moving forward, I was ready to push open the next door. What lay beyond felt unknown, but my experiences had taught me that every challenge could be an opportunity. And so, with hope and a determination to build something meaningful, I stepped forward.

A New Beginning – The Golden Era of My Career

The Perfect Opportunity

After the ups and downs I had faced, stepping back into real estate felt both exciting and daunting, especially after the last 6 months, during which I faced a lot of setbacks rooted in patriarchy and sexism. I was keenly aware that my next steps would shape the future of my career. The success of the plotting project I had undertaken for a friend had given me clarity—it showed me that plotting carried a lower financial risk than residential projects. This realization motivated me to consider starting my own plotting project. If I could manage that successfully, moving on to residential projects would be my next big goal.

To get started, I shared this idea with a trusted friend who had transitioned into development himself. He listened intently, acknowledging the varied experience I had gained over the years—handling land acquisition, legal, drafting of various deeds, sales, CRM, LRM, and even operational aspects. He paused for a moment and then said, "You've got the experience, no doubt. But running a business on your own comes with its own set of challenges. You'll need deeper exposure to understand the full picture before you take that step." His words made sense. I didn't come from a family with a background in real estate, nor did I have their support when it came to matters related to this field. So I knew I couldn't rush this. I needed to find someone who could mentor me, offering the insights that only come with running a business.

The question of who that mentor would be loomed large. My friend even offered me the chance to become a partner in his business. It was a generous and thoughtful gesture, reflecting his belief in my capabilities and my contribution to the project. However, I declined the offer. As I mentioned earlier, I have observed that mixing business relationships with personal or professional bonds often leads to complications. Misaligned expectations, conflicts of interest, and the pressure of shared stakes can strain even the strongest relationships.

I didn't want to risk jeopardizing our friendship by entering into a partnership. For me, preserving the goodwill and mutual respect we had built was more important than taking on a role that could potentially sour the dynamics. This decision wasn't easy, but it was guided by my principles and a clear understanding of the kind of professional environment I wanted to be a part of—one where trust and collaboration could thrive without the complexities of shared ownership.

During this time, I was fortunate to have a network of colleagues and friends who believed in me and supported my decision. My friend, understanding my perspective, stood by me and continued to encourage me from the sidelines. This sense of community, knowing there were people rooting for my success, fueled my confidence.

It was around this period that a significant change in the industry was happening. The Urban Land Ceiling (ULC) Act was nearing its abolition, a move that promised to open up new opportunities for developers. I felt fortunate that my previous work in land acquisition had given me a strong understanding of the ULC Act, including the complexities and legal judgments associated with it. This knowledge became one of my strongest assets as I evaluated my options.

One day, my friend mentioned a small developer who was looking for someone to manage their operations. This developer had already completed two small projects and had a few in the pipeline as well. The role came with appealing perks—a conveniently located office, a car and driver for site visits, and projects not just in Pune but also in a tier-two city in Maharashtra. The opportunity sounded promising but came with its own set of doubts and hesitation from my end, but my friend encouraged me, leaving the final decision up to me.

When I finally decided to meet him, my skepticism was still there, but I was curious, too. As we sat down, our conversation quickly shifted to a land proposal that had been stalled due to issues with the Urban Land Ceiling (ULC) Act. I shared my in-depth understanding of the ULC Act, which I had studied thoroughly, including key High Court and Supreme Court judgments. His eyes lit up—he was genuinely impressed! That initial spark of interest turned our conversation into a deeper discussion.

We talked about everything—my goal of becoming a developer and his ambitious five-year plan. He acknowledged my strengths in land acquisition, drafting, sales, CRM, LRM, and operations but pointed out the areas where I still needed hands-on experience. He highlighted the importance of finance, business strategies, P&L management, target-driven approaches, liaisoning, environmental clearances (a relatively new requirement back then), the MRTP Act, and more. What struck me most was his openness. He suggested we could learn together and even proposed that when I felt ready, I could strike out on my own. This felt different. Could this be the right step forward?

I asked for time to consider the offer. The decision weighed heavily on me, so I did what I always did in times of uncertainty—I went to the Ganesh temple. Having witnessed many life-altering moments in my life, this place was like an anchor, steadying me amidst the chaos as it had many times before. Standing in front of Lord Ganesh, memories of past decisions came flooding back. It felt like a sign, like a green light that said, "Yes, take this chance!"

The next hurdle was convincing my family. They were disheartened by my choice, especially given that I had sold my boutique, which had turned profitable in just two years and had even expanded under its new owner. Their disappointment was palpable, but I stood my ground. I knew deep inside that this was my path. With determination and a clear sense of purpose, I joined the developer's team, even with family opposition. It was a leap, but one I felt ready for. The journey ahead was uncertain, but I knew it was the right step forward.

Taking the Reins

The first few months at the developer's office were a whirlwind. I found myself juggling diverse responsibilities—sales, CRM, and legal work. My background in legal drafting served me well, but I soon realized that I needed to stretch beyond familiar territories. With every passing day, I immersed myself deeper, gradually taking on construction finance and mortgage deeds—areas that had been outside my expertise until then. It was exhilarating! Who would have thought I'd be handling these aspects so confidently? Each new responsibility came with its challenges, but it also brought immense satisfaction.

Expanding my skill set didn't stop there. I soon learned the nuances of Raw TDR, Transfer of Development Rights (TDR) and Development Rights Certificates (DRC) for upcoming projects. This broadened my understanding of how land and construction intersected with regulatory requirements. I found myself absorbing information like a sponge, motivated by the sense of freedom I had to make decisions and lead with initiative. I was so invested in my role that, during this period, I didn't take a single day off. Can you imagine being so driven that work feels more like a passion than a duty? That's exactly how it was! The energy and excitement left little room for anything else.

One of the defining moments during this time was being involved in the booking process of a group of 200 potential buyers. The magnitude of the task was daunting, but I didn't hesitate. This was my chance to step up and show what I was capable of. Guiding this group from their initial booking through to the final possession was a journey marked by intense days, endless problem-solving, and countless late-night calls. But when the last key was handed over, the feeling of accomplishment was overwhelming. It reminded me why I thrived in this industry—the rewards of hard work were tangible and deeply fulfilling. I still vividly remember the possession ceremony of that unique project—it was a day filled with joy and a profound sense of accomplishment. The atmosphere was electric, with everyone radiating happiness as they celebrated the culmination of our hard work and dedication.

The appreciation I received from the company's owner and the customers made the moment even more special. Their heartfelt words of gratitude and admiration validated all the challenges we had overcome to bring this project to life. Seeing the satisfaction on the faces of the new homeowners as they stepped into their dream spaces was truly priceless.

That day wasn't just about handing over keys; it was about delivering promises, building trust, and creating memories for families. The ceremony symbolized the result of countless hours of planning, problem-solving, and teamwork, and it reminded me why I'm so passionate about real estate.

It remains an unforgettable milestone in my career—a moment that reinforced my belief in the value of perseverance and the deep satisfaction of making a tangible impact in people's lives.

Beyond these events, there are some client interactions that stand out in my memory. I recall one particular meeting where a hesitant investor was on the verge of backing out. Through patient listening and understanding his concerns, I was able to reassure him with a detailed plan that met their needs. That conversation turned into a significant deal that boosted our project's credibility.

In this golden era of my real estate journey, I have captured countless such cherished moments that are etched in my memory forever. If I were to write about these moments in detail, I would undoubtedly need to dedicate an entire book to them. From the excitement of land acquisition to the satisfaction of delivering homes, each milestone has added a new dimension to my journey.

I often recall an advertisement from Naukri.com where an employee is being pushed into the office—a depiction of reluctance and lack of motivation. My journey, however, has been the exact opposite. Despite its challenges and the highs and lows along the way, I have never felt the need for someone to push me to work. Real estate is not just my profession; it's my passion. I have enjoyed every moment and every day of my career, immersing myself fully in the dynamic world of this industry.

Yes, there were tough days and a few bad experiences, particularly with colleagues who didn't share the same values or vision. But when I weigh these against the immense knowledge, experience, and fulfillment I've gained, the scale tilts heavily toward the positive. The opportunities to learn, grow, and make a meaningful impact have far outweighed the challenges.

This journey has taught me resilience, shaped my character, and reaffirmed my love for the field. It's a journey I wouldn't trade for anything else—a testament to my unwavering commitment and belief in the potential of this incredible industry.

If there's one thing that has remained constant throughout my journey in real estate, it's my ability to build genuine connections. Whether it's a customer, an investor, or a landowner, there's an immediate sense of trust and rapport when they meet me. This gift of bonding isn't something I consciously cultivated—it's been a natural part of me since my very first job.

I still vividly remember one such incident with an NRI client and his family. He had booked a flat during a pre-launch offer while he was in India and later returned abroad. During a get-together, I had the pleasure of meeting his parents, who were from Bangalore. From that moment, we formed a strong bond, and soon, I started addressing them as Uncle and Aunty. Every time they visited Pune, they made it a point to meet me, even if only for a few minutes. Remarkably, they never once inquired about the status of their son's flat; their visits were purely to connect with me.

One day, they came to the office, but I wasn't there as I had just returned from Mumbai after some official work. Upon learning that I was only 10 minutes away, they called me, mentioning that they were leaving to go abroad and wouldn't be able to meet me for the next 5-6 months. Despite being tired, I couldn't refuse. I got ready and went to meet them at the office.

As usual, I ordered coffee for them, but shortly after, Uncle started feeling uneasy and restless, and Aunty was visibly distressed. Sensing something was seriously wrong, I acted immediately. With the help of my driver and staff, I helped Uncle into the car and rushed him to the nearest hospital. He was having a sudden heart attack.

Aunty was in tears and panicked, so I stayed by her side, reassuring her while keeping their son and daughter updated. Their son was abroad, and their daughter, who lived in Bijapur, needed time to reach Pune. The doctor advised an immediate angioplasty. Without hesitation, I stayed with Aunty at the hospital overnight until their daughter arrived the next day.

That incident deepened our bond. To this day, both their son and daughter remain in touch with me, expressing their gratitude for being there when they needed support the most.

My family, on the other hand, has always been wary of my deep connections in real estate. They felt my involvement went beyond professional boundaries and wanted me to pursue something else. I understand their concerns; their intentions were rooted in care and love. However, I also knew that these relationships were built on trust, sincerity, and compassion—qualities that define who I am.

Real estate, for me, has always been about people, emotions, and making a difference in their lives. This incident, like so many others, reaffirmed why I chose this path and why I continue to stay committed to it.

By the time two years had passed, I had taken on almost every aspect of the business except construction itself. I was leading land acquisitions, liaising with landowners, managing CRM, handling finances, starting a school in one of the projects, and overseeing documentation—the list seemed endless. The team was growing, and so was the company. To top it off, I was given the responsibility of heading a major project in a tier-two city in Maharashtra. That opportunity felt like a testament to how far I'd come.

What I loved most was the independence to make decisions. Routine work bored me—I thrived on challenges, on the unexpected, on the thrill of solving complex problems. Every day felt like a new adventure! This period of my life was more than just about learning skills; it was about understanding what leadership meant to me. It was about proving to myself and others that women can excel in real estate, lead teams, and inspire confidence.

This phase wasn't just professional; it was deeply personal. It solidified my belief that women belong in spaces traditionally reserved for men—and not just to be present but to lead, innovate, and succeed. Those years were filled with achievements, learning, and growth. But the true reward was the confidence it gave me—the belief that this path was where I belonged and that I could excel against any odds.

The Peak of Success

Thinking back to this chapter of my life, it's clear it was a golden era—a time when everything seemed to align perfectly. I had worked hard and taken risks, and now it was paying off in ways I had once only hoped for. Being in the driver's seat was where I thrived; I preferred it more than anything else. The control, the decision-making, the responsibility—it all fueled my ambition and sense of purpose. The decisions I made and the strategies I spearheaded all came together to create something substantial. This phase wasn't just marked by achievements but by the respect I had earned from peers and clients. There was a sense of validation that resonated deeply, not just as a professional but as a leader in a male-dominated field.

Over those four years, the growth I experienced was immeasurable. Each day brought challenges but also victories that fueled my drive. I'd see the tangible results of my work in the projects that took shape and in the trust people placed in me. Leading diverse projects with different sets of challenges taught me lessons that no book or classroom ever could. What stood out most were the acknowledgments I received—clients whom I had once guided through nerve-wracking deals came back, bringing referrals. This word-of-mouth recognition became an important pillar of my career. Moments like these made all the late nights, early mornings, and countless weekend meetings more than worth it.

Over the years, my nature has transformed significantly. I have become more peaceful, patient, and composed in handling challenges. One incident that stands out vividly in my memory exemplifies this change. We had received a notice from the competent authority that could have jeopardized one of our dream projects. An urgent meeting was called, and as I stepped into the boardroom, I found everyone in a state of panic. The tension in the room was palpable, but I remained calm and quiet, carefully analyzing the situation.

The CEO of the company looked at me and remarked, "I don't know how you manage every single situation without missing a beat!" With a smile, I replied, "Every problem has a solution. Some solutions work immediately, while others take time. I may not be a lawyer in a black coat arguing in court, but I believe knowledge and strategy are equally important."

With conviction, I took up the challenge, assuring the CEO that I would lead the initiative to get the notice revoked legitimately within three months. This was more than just a task, it was about safeguarding a project that held immense value for all of us. I channeled my energy into understanding the root of the issue, collaborating with experts, and meticulously working on the resolution.

To everyone's relief and my own satisfaction, the notice was revoked within 60 days—far ahead of the promised timeline. It was a moment of pride, not just for me but for the entire team.

This experience reaffirmed my belief that employees can accomplish remarkable things when their leaders trust and believe in them. Over the years, I've observed that while women employees are often acknowledged for being honest and sincere, very few are openly recognized for their intelligence.

During the golden era of my career, I was fortunate to work with a developer who broke this stereotype. He believed that women are not just diligent but also exceptionally intelligent, capable of leading complex initiatives. His faith in my abilities not only empowered me but also reminded me of the importance of developing an environment where women are seen as equals in talent and intellect.

This journey has been a testament to the power of trust, perseverance, and the belief that challenges are merely opportunities in disguise.

The freedom I had in this role was invigorating! I treated the company as if it were my own, making decisions that weren't always easy but were always aimed at growth. From launching new marketing strategies to creating innovative client experiences, every idea I put forward was met with enthusiasm by a team that shared my ambition. It felt like more than just work; it was a collective pursuit of excellence where everyone was invested in success. Many stakeholders often assumed that I was a partner in the company, primarily because of the level of trust and autonomy I was given to make decisions. I had the freedom to make decisions independently, and over time, my track record spoke for itself—not a single decision I made turned out to be incorrect.

This perception wasn't just a reflection of my role but also a testament to the confidence the leadership had in my abilities. It felt rewarding to know that my judgment was valued and respected, and it motivated me to maintain a high standard of performance.

The freedom to lead and take ownership of critical decisions allowed me to approach challenges with creativity and accountability. Whether it was resolving issues, handling stakeholders, or ensuring smooth project execution, I always prioritized the company's best interests.

This level of responsibility also nurtured my growth as a professional, giving me the confidence to trust my instincts and the discipline to back my decisions with thorough research and strategy. To this day, I cherish the acknowledgment from stakeholders who saw me not just as an employee but as an integral part of the organization's success story.

Recognition? Oh, it came in many forms. Industry peers began noticing my work, and invitations to collaborate on larger, more ambitious projects soon followed. I can still recall the first time I saw my name included in high-level discussions that once felt out of reach—what a surreal feeling! But beyond the public acknowledgment was an even greater reward: the quiet but powerful realization that I truly belonged here. That women could not just be part of real estate but thrive, lead, and inspire change.

Of course, as with any peak, I knew the horizon hinted at challenges to come. This period of success was not the end—I could feel it was just the beginning of something more complex and demanding. The path ahead would have twists and turns, obstacles I couldn't yet see. But with every success, every lesson etched into my memory, I felt more prepared for whatever lay next.

It was during one of those reflective moments that I met with my friend, the same one who once told me to gain experience before setting out on my own. "I'm ready," I said, this time with unwavering conviction. Informing my current boss of my plans wasn't easy; he had been more than a boss—he was a mentor and a supporter. But true to his promise, he stood by me, helping and guiding me as I began transitioning responsibilities. It's incredible to think that the young, eager developer who took a chance on me back then and in whom I saw so much potential is now one of Pune's top developers. Watching his growth over the years has been truly rewarding! It shows how intertwined paths can uplift and elevate those involved.

Those years will always hold a special place in my heart. They shaped not just my career, but my core belief in myself. And as I stood on the edge of the next chapter, filled with excitement and a touch of uncertainty, I knew that this golden era had laid the foundation for all that would come next.

Every year, the core team would gather on January 1st at 1 PM, a symbolic time to set the tone for the year ahead. We would each share our vision and dreams for the company, regardless of whether they were small or grand. The idea was to come together, align our goals, and commit to making those dreams a reality over the course of the year.

Each core member would present their aspirations for their respective departments, and it became a ritual that bonded us all with a shared sense of purpose. For the construction head, the dream was to complete milestones ahead of the planned bar chart, pushing the team to maintain high productivity and efficiency. The sales head would set ambitious goals to sell the unsold inventory, aiming to break records and increase revenue.

These dreams weren't just about numbers or deadlines; they were a reflection of our collective ambition and commitment to taking the company forward. The beauty of this tradition was that it wasn't about competition—it was about cooperation, where every member, regardless of their role, supported the other's goals.

Over the years, this meeting became a cornerstone of our company culture, providing each of us with a sense of ownership over the company's vision. It wasn't just about achieving individual success but about pushing the company toward greater milestones together.

For me, these gatherings were both motivating and humbling, as I saw how each person was deeply invested in the collective success of the company and how every dream, no matter how big or small, had the potential to make a difference.

Those years will always hold a special place in my heart. They shaped not just my career but my core belief in myself. As I stood on the edge of the next chapter, filled with excitement and a touch of uncertainty, I knew that this golden era had laid the foundation for all that would come next. Yet, there was an unspoken feeling in the air, a subtle hint that life was about to change. Just when everything seemed secure, a whisper of tension signaled the need for a pause—an unexpected break that would soon reshape everything I thought I knew about success, balance, and resilience.

Regaining My Ground

The Necessity of a Pause

As I prepared to move forward, I stood firm in my decision to take this journey on my own. After years of dreams, hard work, and careful planning, I had finally secured a piece of land for my plotting project. It was a milestone that represented the culmination of countless efforts and aspirations.

Before stepping away, I had a conversation with my CEO about my decision. Together, we devised a smooth transition plan to ensure everything would be in place. Over the next four months, I focused on wrapping up tasks, preparing my team to take over, and systematically transferring my responsibilities. We had a mutual understanding: whenever the company needed my input, I would be there to assist.

I felt a mix of emotions during this time. On one hand, there was the thrill of venturing into uncharted territory, ready to claim what I had worked so hard for. On the other hand, there was a sense of loss— leaving behind more than just a job. As I sorted through documents, finalized agreements, and mentored my team, I felt the weight of saying goodbye to a part of myself. I would miss the energy of the office, the camaraderie of my colleagues, and the familiar rhythm of my days.

Yet, the excitement for what lay ahead overshadowed any lingering doubt. I was ready to bring my vision to life, to step fully into my new role as a developer. With the land secured and my plans taking shape, I knew I was on the edge of a promising new chapter—one that was entirely my own.

Then, without warning, everything changed.

A personal tragedy struck. There are moments in life that split time into a "before" and an "after," and this was one of those moments. It seemed like a tidal wave crashing in, disturbing everything nearby and making me frantically struggle for air. I didn't see it coming, and the shock rendered me speechless. It felt as if the ground beneath my feet had crumbled away. In a brief instant, all plans and every carefully designed path before me disappeared.

The impact of this disaster was catastrophic. Physically, I felt drained, as if all my energy had been completely exhausted. However, in terms of my mental state—I was coming apart. I always considered myself resilient, someone capable of managing whatever challenges life presented, but this experience left me shattered in a manner I couldn't fully express. At that moment, I felt like I had hit my lowest point, like nothing worse could ever happen to me. There were days when I struggled to leave my bed, nights when sleep seemed like a far-off recollection, and instances when I gazed at the walls, feeling detached from everything around me.

The intensity of the pain exceeded anything I had ever experienced. It felt like a part of me had become mute, and my soul was subdued by the burden of this unexpected grief. The aspirations I had cultivated seemed far away, nearly insignificant, next to the profound void that had taken root inside me. No words appeared sufficient to convey the profound intensity of that emptiness; they felt vacant, like distant echoes of the torment that overwhelmed me. During those days of despair and hopelessness, I found myself looking deep within myself, asking myself and my Ganesh, "Why me?".

My boss, acknowledging the seriousness of the situation, provided me with complete backing. "Take as much time as you need," he said, his tone calm but his eyes filled with understanding. In just eight days, he arranged an early exit for me, tying up all loose ends and ensuring I could leave without any unresolved matters. I hadn't intended to depart so suddenly, but at that time, I lacked the energy to debate or even think about options. I simply realized I had to leave, take a step back and discover a way to understand everything.

During those initial days of my break, I battled with a storm of feelings. There was skepticism, fury, and an overpowering feeling of sorrow. I had dedicated myself to my job and invested all my efforts into creating a future, and now that future was lost—it disappeared in an instant. I found myself doubting everything. How could something so meticulously constructed vanish so swiftly? What remained of my purpose, my motivation, my essential identity? The responses were hard to grasp, and the quest to uncover them seemed infinite.

It wasn't merely the failure of a project or a career goal; it was the disintegration of a vision I had carefully developed over time. I had outlined every aspect and established every step, believing that I held power over my future. Now, everything had vanished, dispersed like dust in the breeze. There was no return to what once was, no recapturing the life I believed I was close to attaining. The subsequent days and weeks were filled with a battle to recover—mentally and physically. My family turned into my support, a lifeline I held onto when all else seemed unstable. They urged me to pursue therapy, understanding that I required more than just time; I had to restore myself from the inside. Therapy turned crucial, a place where I could face the hurt, examine the burden of my losses, and attempt, gradually, to reconstruct myself.

During this mandated break, a difficult reality emerged: our work environment frequently perceives rest with skepticism, as if it were a privilege only available to a select few. Taking a pause, especially in fields fueled by relentless ambition, is viewed as a weakness, as if taking time off somehow lessens your value. As a woman, this stigma seemed even stronger. There's an implicit expectation that women, more than anyone else, must constantly demonstrate their abilities, proving they can maintain their performance without stumbling. Taking a pause, particularly at the peak of one's profession, risks being viewed as ineffective or disengaged.

During my time alone, I struggled with these truths. I reflected on all the years I had devoted to moving ahead, resolved to achieve, never allowing myself to pause. I had always viewed breaks as a privilege, something available to others but not to myself. Now, compelled to take this break, I started to view things in a new light. Rest was not a flaw; it was a vital component of resilience, a time to pause, to recover, to regain energy for the journey ahead. Nevertheless, the world I understood was not built to accept that reality, particularly for women who are expected to work tirelessly without rest.

This extended break over the year turned out to be a life-changing experience, albeit not as I had ever expected. It was an era of unrefined contemplation—a difficult yet essential confrontation with the boundaries of aspiration and the vulnerability of human endurance. I came to understand that the principles upon which I had constructed my career, the relentless pursuit of success and acknowledgment, were delicate and required equilibrium. I discovered, in a profound and painful way, that genuine resilience isn't merely about overcoming every challenge; at times, it involves recognizing when to take a step back and grant yourself the kindness to rest.

During those tranquil times of healing, I gradually started to loosen my hold on the aspirations that had previously taken over my life. I permitted myself to grieve, to dwell in the letdown of unaccomplished plans, to experience the burden of a halted aspiration. In the process, I discovered a different form of strength—a subtle determination not based on accomplishments but on a profound comprehension of my identity, transcending the titles and roles that previously characterized me. During that phase, my family became much more important to me than any dreams and aspirations I have ever had.

This time marked a pivotal moment, an opportunity to evaluate and reconstruct—not with the fervor of my past aspirations but with a softer, more lasting determination. The route I had imagined was lost, yet I was starting to perceive that an alternate way, albeit unclear, stretched out before me. Though I had come to terms with everything and was using this period to reflect, there were moments during that forced break when my nature began to change. I became quite aggressive, and it often affected my mood and interactions. But over time, slowly, I found myself becoming calmer, paving the way to the peaceful and steady person I am today. The break, however difficult, had provided me with something priceless: an opportunity to genuinely grasp resilience, to reimagine strength, and to ready myself, like never before, for the upcoming chapter.

Reentering Real Estate in a New Era

After a year of healing, both mentally and physically, I felt prepared to gradually re-enter the life I had departed from. I understood that beginning anew would be challenging—so much had shifted while I was gone, and I was still burdened by the events that occurred. However, when a longtime colleague/friend, now working as a developer, proposed a role for me overseeing sales and legal for his business, I sensed a spark of optimism. Here stood a well-known figure, someone who recognized my past experiences and what I had achieved prior to my hiatus. The position was nearby and had lesser pay than what I had previously received. Generally, I would not have taken up such an offer to work at a friend's office as it goes against my principles. However, during that phase, it was important for me to be busy, regain my confidence and recall my abilities.

The initial days of returning to an office environment felt unusual. I returned to the field I was familiar with, but everything appeared altered.

As I began to reacquaint myself with the job, it soon became apparent that the industry had undergone a significant change. The introduction of GST and RERA resulted in significant changes, and almost every process I was familiar with was altered by these new rules. It seemed like attempting to master a new language while still communicating with an outdated accent. However, rather than feeling overwhelmed, I experienced a calm resolve. This was a chance to reconnect, update my knowledge, and demonstrate that I could adjust, regardless of how much my surroundings had changed.

Even with my hopefulness, the financial difficulties of my friend's business were clear. The fresh regulations, along with an economy staggering from recent demonetization, indicated that cash flow was constrained, and the whole real estate industry was finding it hard to adapt. This was no longer the stable ground I had previously operated on; it was unstable and uncertain. Still, I became thoroughly engaged and resolved to contribute to my friend's business and help it survive. I immersed myself in each project and challenge, experiencing a revived sense of purpose, even if it was in a different role than prior.

However, as the months went by, it became evident that the burden of the industry's challenges was overwhelming. The financial pressure kept increasing, and despite everyone's hard work, he ultimately had to sell his office, and the staff stopped coming to work. And just like that, I encountered yet another pause, compelled to withdraw from a career I had only just started to regain.

In contrast to the initial break, which had been emotionally intense and intimate, this one was characterized by a subdued sense of disappointment and persistent frustration. I returned to the industry, aiming to regain the passion and purpose I previously experienced, but found myself beginning anew once more. It seemed like an infinite loop of attempting to get to the top, only to be dragged back down. Following this setback, I had to face an undeniable truth: my career, which was previously rising, had experienced a decline. The "golden era" felt like a faded recollection, and although I had reached remarkable achievements, I couldn't shake the unsettling sense that I had somehow strayed from my path. That insight was hurtful.

However, rather than allowing it to drag me down, it turned into a strong source of motivation. I wasn't prepared to abandon my aspirations, but I realized I needed to fortify myself if I was going to endure upcoming challenges. To stay busy and fully utilize this unanticipated break, I immersed myself in studying. During this period, RERA was operating at its peak, reshaping the industry by emphasizing regulation and accountability. I chose to enroll in a RERA course at law school to enhance my knowledge of the act's influence on real estate. If I intended to return to the field, I aimed to be ready and knowledgeable in all facets of the new regulations.

Besides RERA, I obtained my Yellow and Green Belts in Lean Six Sigma. Having a focus on processes has consistently been one of my strengths, and I viewed this as a chance to enhance my skills even more. It was exhilarating to transform my frustration into a productive effort, one that would eventually be advantageous for me over time. I was collecting tools, preparing myself for the next stage, whatever it could entail.

However, an unmistakable feeling of sorrow was present at this stage. When you cling to a goal with great intensity, only to have situations repeatedly push it out of reach, it impacts you in a certain way. There were moments when I wondered why I continued to strive, why I didn't simply abandon the dream completely. The disappointment weighed heavily, serving as a constant reminder of the fragility of our plans. Yet, even during my darkest times, a faint voice within continued to encourage me to persevere. Perhaps this was simply another diversion, another segment of the journey I hadn't foreseen.

Throughout this time, I also undertook a minor project for a friend who required assistance with registering his properties under RERA.

I worked remotely, immersing myself in the regulations with a concentration that felt oddly reassuring. It felt as if the work served as an anchor, a reminder that I still had value to contribute, that I still comprehended this world, even though it had transformed. Gradually, I successfully obtained RERA certificates for each of his projects, managing all aspects independently. That minor achievement gave me a feeling of pride I hadn't experienced in some time. It served as a reminder that, even when situations appear intent on bringing you down, there are consistently minor triumphs to discover.

Through this work, I could see just how much the real estate landscape had transformed. Demonetization, RERA, GST—it was a different world from the one I had once thrived in. And just as the industry had evolved, so had I. This second break became a time of recalibration, a chance to let go of rigid expectations and allow myself to go with the flow, taking each day as it came. Instead of feeling pressured to follow a linear path, I embraced the beauty of taking things one step at a time.

Looking back on my experiences during this time, I remember the enthusiasm that had previously motivated me. My aspiration to become a doctor and later a developer stemmed not from the chase of fame or wealth—but from a true passion for impactful work, for the challenges and satisfaction it provided. That enthusiasm was still present, but I started to understand that its manifestation might require adaptation. Medicine may have been unattainable, but real estate? That remained within my reach.

As I prepared to re-enter the field, I recognized that the path ahead would not be easy. However, I acquired something priceless throughout this period: a revitalized sense of patience and the realization that setbacks are not just barriers—they're integral to the journey. This wasn't merely about advancing without thought; it was about true resilience, involving moments of pause, contemplation, and the bravery to start anew.

A Fateful Conversation

While I was finding my footing again in real estate, an unforeseen meeting revealed an entirely new viewpoint. A senior family member contacted me, seeking assistance in purchasing a property in a prominent Mumbai development. Due to our strong relationship, I was pleased to help by organizing a meeting with the developer and joining him to settle the details. What I expected to be a brief, simple chat unexpectedly evolved into an in-depth, hour-long dialogue about real estate. We discussed the changes in the industry, the insights I had gained, and the obstacles I had encountered. It was refreshing to discuss my experiences with someone who grasped the industry's intricacies.

As our discussion came to an end, he gazed at me contemplatively and remarked, "You possess a wealth of experience and numerous insights." "Why not write something regarding real estate?" His remarks stayed with me long after we departed. Writing and reading have always been my personal interests, but I never considered capturing my real estate experience. Yet, here was an esteemed individual proposing that my experiences could be valuable to share. It felt as though he had ignited a flame, triggering a thought I hadn't known existed. Can I truly express my thoughts verbally? The idea of it awakened something within me. Maybe by telling my story, I would discover a different type of purpose.

In the following weeks, I began to write, expressing my ideas on paper for my personal enjoyment. As I penned my thoughts, I started outlining the evolution of real estate as I had observed it—from my initial experiences in the field to the profound transformations it had experienced. My investigation grew comprehensive, encompassing policies and significant incidents from HUDCO to PMAY, ULC, the effects of SEZs, the 2008 financial downturn, the LARR Act, and more recently, RERA, GST, and the Insolvency and Bankruptcy Code and many more. Every moment I seized was beyond mere reality; it was a memory, a testament to how profoundly real estate had influenced me throughout the years. This project occupied my time, providing a sense of purpose, but a persistent unease still lingered. Real estate grew into a passion as deep as my original aspiration to pursue medicine. Now, after taking a break, I understood just how much I longed to be involved.

This thorough exploration of my journey led to a significant moment of self-reflection. Why had I desired to become a doctor and, subsequently, a developer? It wasn't for fame or riches. It has always centered on passion—a desire to engage in something significant, something that would inspire my spirit daily. That understanding struck me deeply. Healthcare had become inaccessible, but property? Real estate was present, and I still had a lot to offer it. What about the concept of the title "Doctor"? Perhaps, just perhaps, there was still a means to fulfill that dream.

The idea of seeking a Ph.D. crossed my mind, initially like a subtle whisper. Lacking a solid strategy, I began to investigate, reaching out to different universities with my suggestion. I envisioned academia as a continuation of my path, a method to leave a permanent impact on the discipline. However, every meeting confronted me with the same doubt and skepticism—concerns regarding the significance of real estate as a field deserving of scholarly examination. Most provided subjects, such as physics or chemistry, cannot recognize real estate as a legitimate area for thorough examination. Every rejection hurt, yet I persevered. I came to understand that this journey was transforming into more than merely earning a degree; it was about affirming my experiences, my insights, and my conviction that real estate impacted lives and industries in ways that many people did not fully comprehend.

Resolute in my quest to progress, I sought out fresh starts in different places. I desired a new beginning, preferably in a location where I wouldn't be recognized or interrogated about my previous positions—a space where I could concentrate solely on the tasks, unburdened by former expectations. I contacted a career consultant I relied on, and she told me about a job with a developer. The position was significantly different from what I had experienced before, and it didn't directly report to the owner as my past roles did, but I chose to give it a try.

I can still recall my initial encounter with the young CEO. He possessed an unmistakable brilliance—a forward-thinking perspective that brought to mind my own "golden age." I experienced an immediate bond with his enthusiasm and passion. He talked about his dreams with such passion that I couldn't help but feel motivated. Though they were always against me being involved in real estate, when I talked about the offer with my family, they consented, considering my state of mind back then. However, they did so under the condition that I would depart within a year to prevent the lengthy commute. Even though the distance wasn't perfect, I realized this was a chance worth seizing.

Right from the beginning, I was reminded that there is always something fresh to discover. Even with my extensive experience, I felt motivated by the innovative mindset of this youthful group. The owner's family brought back memories of my initial experiences in the industry, where people were tightly connected, down-to-earth, and driven by true passion instead of accolades or status. Collaborating with them made me feel as though I had returned to an era when real estate was motivated by goals and inspiration rather than merely financial gains.

As the months progressed into years, I realized I was advancing swiftly. In just a few months, I transitioned to a higher role. It served as a reminder that when someone has faith in you, growth occurs effortlessly. Advancements occurred quickly, not due to tenure, but because my input was acknowledged and appreciated. The atmosphere was supportive, and I sensed that well-known flame rekindling inside me.

A year later, my family started pushing me to stop going because of the commute. Although it was far away, I kept going because the position had provided me with so much. I had rejuvenated the core of my profession, rekindled my enthusiasm, and restored my self-assurance. This phase wasn't merely another position; it represented a chapter that enabled me to appreciate the journey, recognizing that each obstacle and every unforeseen twist had guided me to this state of equilibrium and satisfaction.

Reflecting on it now, that spontaneous chat with my family member about helping him buy a flat triggered a series of events I could never have foreseen. It wasn't merely a suggestion from the developer to write; it was an invitation to explore my narrative again, to discover meaning in every twist and turn I had faced. During this journey, I discovered that often, the most significant moments emerge from the most unexpected sources. As I stood at the brink of yet another fresh start, I felt prepared—prepared to welcome whatever lay ahead, with a greater insight into what truly counted.

A Tale of Two Doctorates

A Turning Point in Uncertain Times

In the years before 2020, I had been pushing myself in every conceivable manner. My days were full, my timetable unyielding, with almost ten hours a day dedicated to work and a tiring commute on top of it. The office was far from my home, and my family became increasingly worried as they observed the extensive time I was away from home and the impact it was having on me. However, to me, every day seemed like a move toward the future I was resolved to create. I wanted to stay busy with work, to feel productive and focused, even if it came at the cost of my personal time. I assured myself that the extended hours were only for a while and that the sacrifices would eventually yield results. Thus, I continued, persuading myself that I could manage everything as long as I stayed focused and moved ahead.

Subsequently, in March 2020, everything transformed. The planet faced the COVID-19 pandemic—an unseen, silent power that caused life to come to a standstill. Roads cleared, workplaces shut, and silence fell over the world. For the first time, it seemed as if time had halted, allowing all of us to confront our thoughts, our worries, and the abrupt awareness of how delicate life really is. This confinement compelled me to meet myself, to address the silent thoughts I had been evading. Initially, I attempted to remain occupied, holding onto the habits that had previously organized my existence. Yet, as the days melded into weeks, I began to confront something more profound, something that had been accumulating long before the pandemic.

Just before the pandemic, I had already started to withdraw a bit, a change brought on by the deeply personal experience that had left its mark on me. After that painful incident, I began pulling back from the social life I once thrived in. I had always been someone who loved gatherings, catching up with friends, meeting colleagues—those 4-5 meet-ups a month were something I genuinely looked forward to. But suddenly, after everything that happened, that same joy wasn't there. I found myself withdrawing, craving solitude where there had once been a need for connection. It wasn't easy to admit, even to myself, that something in me had shifted, that the lightness I once felt was harder to reach. That experience had left scars I wasn't quite sure how to heal, and now, with the world in lockdown, I found myself alone with those lingering questions and quiet fears.

Then came a call that I'll never forget. It was an old friend from my very first corporate job, someone who knew the younger, eager version of me who thought anything was possible. He had reached out to check in, asking how my family was managing through the pandemic, and there was something comforting in that call—a brief moment that pulled me back to memories of simpler times. He mentioned he had recently left his corporate life to start something entirely new, something that brought him joy and peace. He had bought a small plot of land and taken up organic farming, a passion he had carried quietly for years. Hearing him talk about this dream he was living felt like a breath of fresh air. It reminded me that sometimes, we don't have to let go of our dreams; we just have to find the right time to make them real.

We didn't speak for long—only a few minutes—but as we ended the call, I felt uplifted, even optimistic. I wished him well, assuring him I would keep in contact. However, life, as is frequently the case, had its own intentions. Merely a week later, I got the news that he had died from COVID-19. I was shocked. I recall being there, phone in my grasp, sensing the heaviness of his absence enveloping me. It felt like the world had fallen silent once more, and within that quiet, a harsh truth struck me: aspirations, intentions, all that we cling to—everything can disappear in an instant.

That evening, I found myself alone, unable to dismiss the feeling of conclusion. I reflected on his words, his enthusiasm for the life he was creating, and the harsh truth that he would never witness it develop. It served as a reminder I couldn't overlook—a reminder of life's fragility and how quickly it can fade if we allow it to. I realized, at that instant, that I needed to confront my own aspirations, the ones I had been postponing for "later." I could no longer allow them to disappear into the background. I didn't want to someday reflect and find only unmet dreams and incomplete ambitions.

So, I pulled out a notebook and started to write. I listed the dreams that had been with me since I was young. The first was to become a doctor—a dream I had set aside years ago but one that still held a special place in my heart. The second was to be a real estate developer, to create something that would stand the test of time. But looking at those dreams on paper, they felt so far away. Circumstances, family responsibilities, practicalities—all these reasons kept reminding me why they seemed out of reach.

I gazed at that list, experiencing a blend of desire and disillusionment. Yet I couldn't dismiss the voice within me that urged, "Don't quit." These weren't merely fresh concepts or far-off aspirations—I had thought about seeking a PhD during times when everything felt beyond my control while I was attempting to gather the shattered fragments of my life. At that time, the idea of academia had come to me quietly, like a soft suggestion, a way to leave a mark on an industry I loved deeply. I had reached out to universities, met with advisors, and tried to propose a research focus that spoke to my passion for real estate. But every step forward had been met with skepticism; real estate, they said, wasn't a subject suited to the level of academic exploration I envisioned. It had been disheartening, facing rejection after rejection, but I hadn't given up. The dream had lingered.

Now, in this reflective quiet of lockdown, that same dream surfaced again, but this time with a deeper, unwavering sense of purpose. I wasn't just entertaining the idea anymore—I was determined to push through, no matter what. If I couldn't find a path, I would carve one. I couldn't keep setting my aspirations aside; the pursuit of this PhD had become more than an academic goal. It was a declaration of resilience, a testament to my belief in this journey, and a commitment to seeing it through, even when the odds weren't in my favor.

Taking the First Steps Towards the PhD

In May 2020, the world was still locked down, and I was finding my way through quiet reflections. One day, I received a call that felt like fate. It was from the executive assistant of the same developer from Mumbai who had encouraged me to write about my experiences in real estate. His words had planted a seed in me, stirring ideas and prompting me to write. Now, his assistant was calling, and he connected me to the developer who wanted to check on my progress. This was a thoughtful follow-up that surprised me. This wasn't just another routine call—someone out there had genuinely cared enough to see if I'd started the journey he had inspired.

As we spoke, I could feel a familiar excitement bubbling up within me, and without a second thought, I started talking about my dream of earning a PhD. I told him about the topic I'd carefully perfected over the last couple of years: Evolving Dynamics of the Real Estate Market in India: A Comprehensive Analysis from 1998 to Present. When he realized the depth of my passion, he put me directly in touch with the Vice-Chancellor of a renowned management school and research center, and after a few discussions with their team, I was offered the chance to apply for their PhD program. This was the opportunity I had been waiting for! Could I really do it, though? I was 43—wasn't it too late to start something like this? My heart raced with the thought of going back to school, of diving into something entirely new, with a world of young minds and fresh perspectives all around me.

The thought felt thrilling and terrifying all at once, but I knew I couldn't let this chance pass me by. After passing the entrance exam, I was officially beginning a new chapter—a commitment I knew would be nothing short of transformative. I'd spoken with a counselor early on who had given me a piece of advice that would stay with me through each step. He told me, "This journey is not just about a degree—it's about rediscovering parts of yourself and challenging what you thought you knew. It's going to be life-changing if you let it be." And he was right; this wasn't simply an academic pursuit, it was a path that would test, shape, and stretch me in ways I hadn't anticipated.

Distinct from any other type of study I've encountered, a PhD is an independent pursuit—a solitary path where no one else determines the speed or offers the solutions. There's no "guidance" here, no organized curriculum to adhere to. Rather, there is the liberty to investigate, coupled with the significant obligation to delve deeper than ever prior. At times, this freedom was thrilling, yet at other moments, it felt burdensome, nearly overwhelming to handle. I would wonder, "Am I insane for doing this?" But the spark that had driven me toward this goal kept me going. I realized that the very thing I feared—going back to academia at 43, balancing a family, a career, and this immense personal goal—was what made this journey so deeply meaningful.

The first hurdles were real. I found myself juggling work demands with study hours, wondering if I had taken on more than I could handle. There were nights when I questioned myself when exhaustion from the day left me staring blankly at a page, not even sure if I was making any sense. But then I'd remember the fire that had brought me here, the quiet promise I'd made to myself when I sat down and wrote out my dreams.

This PhD wasn't just about a title or even about a field of expertise; it was about resilience, about facing my own limitations and finding new ways to push past them.

Each step forward reminded me that this wasn't just about the degree waiting at the end. It was about discovering who I could become through this process, about building the strength to tackle challenges I hadn't foreseen, and finding out that even in the face of doubt, I could take one more step forward. This was a journey that would test my resolve, but it was also the journey I had chosen, one that allowed me to reconnect with my passion for learning and growth, even after all these years. I knew I was exactly where I was meant to be.

The Doctoral Journey: Progress, Struggles, and Sacrifices

Once the excitement of starting the PhD settled in, the reality of the path ahead began to sink in. My days quickly filled with tasks that, on the surface, seemed straightforward—literature reviews, planning my research, developing frameworks—but each step was more intense than I had anticipated. There was a thrill in diving into something I loved, but balancing my study goals with the commitments of family and work was a different kind of challenge. I remember sitting with my notebook late into the night, mapping out timelines and strategies, hoping to find a rhythm that would let me move forward without sacrificing too much in either direction.

The journey began in earnest with the research and planning phase, an essential step that required me to lay a strong foundation for everything that was to follow. Developing a proposal, refining my research question, and finding the right mentor was like building a roadmap. At first, the task felt daunting, but each completed step reminded me why I'd started this journey. I kept thinking of how my work could add to the field I was so passionate about. Real estate had been my career for years, and here was a chance to understand it on a completely new level! I was driven by the desire not only to answer my research questions but also to honor the journey itself.

As I moved into the literature review, I discovered just how complex my field truly was. Going through decades of studies and analyses, identifying gaps in knowledge, and building a theoretical framework—these tasks pushed me to my intellectual limits. Some days, I'd close the books feeling exhilarated, as if I'd unearthed a new piece of wisdom that could change everything. On other days, I felt lost in a sea of information, wondering if I was piecing things together correctly. The sheer depth of the literature amazed me, but it also kept me grounded. I was joining a conversation that had begun long before me, and it was humbling to think of my work as a small contribution to this vast academic dialogue.

With a solid framework in place, I moved on to collecting and analyzing data—a stage that demanded not just attention to detail but immense patience. Gathering data, scheduling interviews, ensuring unbiased results, and refining my methodology were intricate tasks that tested my focus daily. There were times I felt overwhelmed, moments when the endless spreadsheets, numbers, and notes began to blur together. Yet each insight I gained, each trend that began to emerge, reminded me of why I was here. I found purpose in knowing that these details would shape the findings I'd eventually present to the world.

Balancing these responsibilities with my family life, work demands, and personal well-being wasn't easy. I created a rigorous schedule, setting aside dedicated hours each day—early mornings and late evenings became study times, while Sundays turned into research marathons. My family, always my greatest source of support, adapted to this new routine, understanding the late nights, the missed dinners, and the countless weekends I devoted to this goal. But the mental strain was real. There were times I questioned myself, especially when the workload felt too heavy and when progress seemed painstakingly slow. "Is this worth it? Can I really handle this?" I would wonder. Yet, each time I thought about stopping, I would remember why I'd started. I wanted to create something meaningful, something my sons could one day look at with pride.

Alongside the research, there were other responsibilities that came with pursuing a PhD. Conferences, workshops, and publishing papers added another layer to the experience. These opportunities enriched my understanding, broadened my network, and allowed me to contribute to discussions in my field. Though each of these events required preparation, they helped me stay connected with my profession and made me feel like I was making strides, however small. With each paper I presented and each discussion I joined, I felt a growing sense of purpose, as if I was slowly finding my place in the academic world.

Writing the thesis itself was a test of endurance, requiring not just knowledge but discipline. Translating years of work into a cohesive, comprehensive narrative was both daunting and exhilarating. I faced countless bouts of writer's block, times when the words just wouldn't come, when the weight of years' worth of research felt impossible to capture. But with each chapter, I felt a sense of accomplishment, a tangible reflection of my journey. Editing, proofreading, reworking sections—this was a cycle I went through repeatedly, striving to make my work clear, concise, and impactful.

There were days when exhaustion gnawed at me when I felt as though my ambition was outpacing my abilities. I'd ask myself questions that lingered long into the night: What if I failed? What if the time and resources I had invested ended in disappointment? What if my sons, watching me, saw a mother who reached for something too high only to fall short? These thoughts weren't easy to face, but each time they surfaced, I returned to the promise I'd made to myself. I wanted to be the kind of example my sons could look up to, someone who persisted despite the odds and who showed them that dreams were worth fighting for.

Then came the final hurdle, defending my research. Standing before a committee, presenting my findings, and answering questions—it was nerve-wracking and fulfilling all at once. Every late night, every challenge, every moment of doubt had led to this. Defending my work was about more than just proving my research's validity; it was a validation of my journey, a moment that made every struggle worthwhile.

Of course, this journey wasn't without its sacrifices. Adapting to a new academic environment at my age meant overcoming self-doubt, learning how to juggle work responsibilities with academic demands, and navigating financial commitments that sometimes felt overwhelming. To avoid distractions at work, I had kept my PhD pursuit largely private, working quietly on my goals without drawing attention. This approach helped me avoid the pitfalls of premature scrutiny, but it also meant bearing the weight of these goals on my own shoulders.

As the PhD journey unfolded, a new possibility entered my mind—a Global Doctor of Business Administration (GDBA) degree. Around a year into my PhD, a cousin who had moved to Switzerland mentioned the GDBA program at the Swiss School of Business Management. Unlike the PhD, which dives deeply into theoretical research, the GDBA was more practical and grounded in real-world applications. The idea intrigued me. Would a dual-degree path grant me an even broader perspective, allowing me to connect my academic pursuits with industry insights? The thought was enticing, promising a fusion of theoretical knowledge with practical expertise, something that could offer even greater relevance in the global arena.

I didn't have all the answers, but one thing was clear: this journey was about more than just earning a title. It was about resilience, growth, and leaving behind a legacy—not just for myself but for my family, my sons, and those who would come after me.

Pursuing Two Doctorates: A Testament to Resilience

The idea of pursuing two doctorates, let alone managing the PhD itself, felt both thrilling and overwhelming. Yet, as I looked at the possibilities, a Global Doctorate in Business Administration (GDBA) seemed like the next logical step, a way to bridge my academic pursuits with practical, global insights. While my PhD centered on real estate, this GDBA would focus on something more versatile—Customer Relationship Management (CRM). However, choosing a research topic was no small feat. I'd initially thought of CRM specifically within Indian real estate, but my counselor quickly pointed out, "If you want this to resonate globally, it needs a wider scope."

It was a fair challenge, and after some thought, I decided on "Quantitative Analysis of Customer Relationship Management: Concepts and Importance," examining CRM across industries from finance to retail, healthcare, and tech. This broader focus felt more like uncharted territory, taking me outside my comfort zone of real estate and into industries I hadn't studied in depth before. But I knew that if I wanted to grow, I had to embrace this challenge wholeheartedly.

Adjusting to the international academic environment at the Swiss School of Business and Management was daunting. Unlike my familiar setting in India, I was now navigating new expectations, approaches, and even nuances in communication. My mentor from Griffith University provided a steady hand, guiding me not just academically but through the subtle shifts in approach, down to pronunciations that felt foreign to me at first. My family, too, reacted with a mix of surprise and excitement—after years in real estate, here I was, expanding my academic reach to global CRM. It felt like a new chapter in more ways than one!

Balancing both the PhD and GDBA was another story altogether. My schedule became relentless—early mornings were dedicated to my PhD research, evenings and Sundays to the GDBA. Weekends became study marathons, my desk a familiar sight as dawn turned to dusk. Yet, even amid this organized chaos, there were days when exhaustion would creep in, days when I'd question my sanity in choosing two such intensive paths at once. "Why am I putting myself through this?" I'd wonder. But deep down, I knew. This journey was about so much more than titles or academic credentials. It was about growth, resilience, and proving to myself that I could overcome any barrier life threw my way.

Then, in 2022, life threw a new challenge my way. I was diagnosed with a serious health issue, the kind that would normally demand a complete halt. Family members and doctors encouraged me to take it easy, to set my studies aside, if only temporarily. But I couldn't bring myself to step back, not when I had come so far. I chose a hospital close to home, making it easier to manage treatments without disrupting my study routine. Even during recovery, my books were my companions. Each study session was a reminder of why I had embarked on this journey— to learn, to grow, and to prove that I could keep going, no matter the obstacles.

In August 2023, my PhD adventure concluded successfully. Following years of tireless work, numerous nights without sleep, and instances when I questioned, "Will this ever happen?" I have finally received the title "Dr." Can you picture the relief? It seemed unreal. A dream I had cherished for countless years was now a reality. While I grasped my degree, a smile crept onto my face. It wasn't merely a sheet of paper. It represented everything I had labored for, wept over, and given up. The burden I had borne for such a long time, the uncertainties, the anxiety, the fatigue, was finally lifted. I was able to breathe freely once more.

Earning the highest degree proved to be even more rewarding than I had anticipated. I expected it to feel amazing, but it was vastly beyond that. It was profoundly intimate, a tribute to my strength, resolve, and steadfast faith in myself. I experienced pride rising within me, along with a sense of gratitude. Thankfulness to everyone who supported me, for every difficulty that strengthened me, and for the part of myself that persevered.

But then came the reactions from others, and they weren't all what I expected. Some people truly celebrated with me, and their congratulations were filled with warmth and sincerity. Those moments felt amazing as if my joy was reflected in their eyes. Yet, others were different. Their words were laced with sarcasm or indifference. "Oh, so you're a doctor now? We'd better watch out!" someone joked. "Sure, she has a doctorate, but does she know how things work in real life?" another muttered. How do you respond to that? At first, I didn't know. Those comments lingered in my mind, dulling the shine of the moment a little, a tinge of sadness trying to overpower the jubilation I had been feeling.

And then there was the industry's reaction, or, more accurately, the lack of one. I had thought earning this degree would change everything. I imagined that doors would open wider and that my work would be viewed with newfound respect. But the reality was quieter than I had hoped. That was hard to come to terms with, and to be honest, it hurt. However, this is what I realized. The world doesn't always acknowledge your achievements in the manner you anticipate, and that's perfectly fine. This was not concerning them. This title was not merely about the letters preceding my name or seeking outside approval. It was about demonstrating something to myself. It was a vow I had taken years earlier, and I fulfilled it. That's what was important. Reflecting on the past, I wouldn't alter a single aspect. Indeed, the trip was lengthy and exhausting. Indeed, the responses were not always what I desired. However, this PhD belongs to me. It stands as evidence of determination, reflecting the nights I felt like quitting but chose not to, showcasing a resilience I was unaware I possessed. Each time I notice "Dr." in front of my name, it brings to mind the passion within me that continued to blaze even when everything around me felt bleak. To me, that holds greater value than any applause.

And the adventure wasn't over. Only a year later, I finished my GDBA with an A+ grade. At that moment, I experienced a blend of satisfaction and pride that no one could undermine. I had achieved it—I finished not just one but two doctorate degrees, an accomplishment I never imagined could happen when I started this academic path. Some individuals responded with congratulations, while others remained just as indifferent as they had been. However, I wasn't concerned this time. I was aware of my achievements. Each degree represented not only my dedication but also the steadfast encouragement of my family, the silent sacrifices they endured, and the resilience I developed, overcoming challenges gradually.

My mentor had once anticipated that life following the attainment of the doctorate would change, and he was correct. Reflecting on the past, I perceive a path that encompassed far more than just academic success— it was a voyage of resilience, flexibility, and personal development. I balanced work obligations, managed the challenges of motherhood, handled workplace politics, and ultimately obtained not just one but two doctorates. With every obstacle and each restless night, I discovered a refreshed sense of patience, a greater appreciation for persistence, and a significant respect for the strength of gradual, consistent efforts.

To everyone who meets a person with a doctorate, I wish for you to look past the title. Keep in mind that every degree signifies not just knowledge but also a narrative of determination, discipline, and the sacrifices endured. It serves as a reminder that, regardless of the challenges, determination can lead us through the bleakest times. For me, this journey has served as a reminder that each small step forward carries significance. With each degree obtained and every challenge encountered, I've realized that resilience is more than just a characteristic—it's a lifestyle.

The Second Innings

Life After the Doctorate

When I finally received my PhD in Real Estate, my immediate thought was to contact the person who had faith in my abilities long before I recognized them myself—the developer who motivated me to begin writing initially. His remarks, delivered with such nonchalance in our chat, had awakened something profound inside me, inspiring me to take a step I never imagined I could. I called his number, experiencing a blend of excitement and gratitude, and as soon as he picked up, I instantly had to share the news with him. His response was precisely what I had anticipated—authentic pride and support. He promptly invited me to come to his office and bring my thesis with me.

Upon entering his office, I recognized this was not a typical meeting. Here was a man recognized for his keen perceptions, and even with his hectic agenda, he took a seat and started reading my thesis immediately, completely absorbed. He didn't merely glance at it; he turned every page deliberately, occasionally stopping to take in the details. For almost three hours, it went on in quiet reverence as he examined my work. I recall being there, experiencing a mix of anxious excitement and great pride. Here was an individual I truly admired, investing time to grasp every detail of what I had devoted my heart to. Once he finished, he gazed at me with a look that conveyed so much—a glance that recognized the extensive path I had traveled to arrive here.

Then, in a simple yet powerful gesture, he called in his executive assistant and presented me with a pen. It wasn't just any pen; it was a symbol of recognition, a quiet acknowledgment of my hard work and resilience. In his world, where every gesture carried meaning, this was a sign of respect, an indication that he saw me as an equal. And at that moment, as I accepted the pen and took his blessings for my future, I felt a profound sense of gratitude. This wasn't just about the title "Doctor"; it was about the journey it took to get here, the belief he had placed in me, and the satisfaction of knowing I had honored that belief.

During my Doctorate journey, I had a conversation with the HR person about the selection process for a potential candidate. Our discussion took a turn when she casually remarked, "In this industry, experience often matters more than degrees." Her comment was not directed at me, but it stayed with me nonetheless. Real estate, I realized, often values practical, hands-on experience far more than formal education. This wasn't entirely surprising, but it still made me pause and think. I had invested years into earning my degrees, believing they were the ultimate key to success. Yet here was the reality—degrees alone didn't always carry the weight I had imagined.

That conversation didn't discourage me, though. If anything, it strengthened my belief in the power of education. For me, education is about much more than qualifications; it's about shaping critical thinking, understanding the "why" behind decisions, and cultivating a mindset that drives innovation. At the same time, I acknowledged the industry's emphasis on results and action. It wasn't about choosing between education and experience—they were two sides of the same coin.

Instead of dwelling on the disparity, I let it motivate me. This conversation was a reminder that while experience might carry weight in real estate, education was my anchor. I saw it as a tool to enhance my skills and stay adaptable, which determined me to focus on continuous professional development during this period.

After the completion of my degree, the gates opened to new possibilities and opportunities. Fueled by my drive to pursue further education and determined to achieve more personal growth, I immersed myself in professional certifications during this period. My Lean Six Sigma Yellow and Green Belt certifications were completed just before the pandemic, and I earned my Black Belt afterward, dedicating a year to mastering it while continuing my job. I also pursued a Train-the-Trainer course focused on the POSH Act and diversity, as well as certification in mediation. These weren't just resume-builders for me—they were ways to stay engaged, challenge myself, and remain relevant in an ever-changing professional environment.

For instance, the POSH certification held personal significance. When I first completed my law degree, the POSH Act wasn't even in place. However, as the workplace evolved, I realized how essential it was to understand and advocate for safe and equitable environments. Becoming a certified external POSH advisor wasn't just about staying relevant; it was about ensuring I could make meaningful contributions in spaces that needed it the most.

Expanding Skills and Networks

As I grew into my role, I noticed a common thread running through my work—I was often called upon to mediate, to resolve, to bring people together. Conflict resolution had become a natural skill, one I'd honed through countless meetings, negotiations, and long conversations, and my life mentor, a retired High Court judge, saw it, too. "You're good at navigating people's differences," he observed one day. "Why not make it an expertise?" His words stayed with me, igniting a curiosity I hadn't expected. Was this skill something I could master even further? Was there more I could bring to the table if I turned this talent into a formal qualification?

I followed his advice, immersing myself in an intensive course on Alternate Dispute Resolution. The journey wasn't just academic; it was a reintroduction to the very core of what it means to resolve conflict with integrity and fairness. By the end, I'd earned an award for excellence in arbitration writing—a proud moment, no doubt, but even more, a testament to the guidance and belief of someone who'd seen potential in me before I saw it myself. Each time I apply those skills now, I remember his words, feeling grounded in the knowledge that I'm carrying forward a legacy of integrity in conflict resolution.

Amid this growth, an opportunity arose from a place I hadn't anticipated. A friend from college, now an actor and a passionate advocate for social causes, reached out. He'd launched an organization to support farmers—a cause close to his heart but one that lacked structure and stability. Could I help? His new team needed someone to establish a system and bring order, where there was now only enthusiasm but little direction.

How could I say no? It wasn't just a request for help; it was a chance to contribute to something truly meaningful. I committed my Sundays, knowing this was more than a logistical task—it was a purpose. Over the next three months, I dedicated four hours each weekend to creating processes that would support his team's growth. The work wasn't glamorous, but seeing the impact was deeply fulfilling. With a solid framework in place, the organization started to thrive, and my friend was overjoyed. His gratitude was palpable, and I knew that, in helping his team, I had reignited my own sense of purpose. This was a reminder that when we give freely, the rewards come back in ways we never expect.

Amid all this, I also joined a prestigious national real estate organization. It was a refreshing change, interacting with senior developers from across the country who not only recognized my knowledge but also respected it. This was starkly different from some of the dismissive attitudes I had encountered earlier. Their validation reignited a part of me that had gone quiet—I began to rediscover my confidence and, gradually, my social side, which I had suppressed for so long.

This chapter of my life became a bridge, preparing me for the opportunities and decisions that would soon come my way. Each certification, every connection, and every small step forward strengthened my foundation, leading me toward the next exciting phase of my journey.

One day, I came across the National Real Estate Organization, a network of incredibly talented women from every corner of the industry—architects, landscape designers, developers, each one bringing her expertise to the field. I knew instantly that I wanted to be part of this community, to connect with women who understood not only the technical demands of our work but the unspoken challenges we encounter daily. I soon had the chance to interview with the president, and to my delight, I was welcomed into this national network.

Being part of this group was like finding a new source of energy. Each conversation and each connection brought fresh perspectives, and it became clear that this was more than networking; it was a lifeline of inspiration and solidarity. These women had each fought their own battles, and together, we were redefining what it meant to be professionals in this industry. How powerful is that? I was surrounded by people who not only understood my journey but also lived it. In every meeting, I felt a renewed motivation, a reminder that I wasn't alone on this path.

Looking back, I realize that this whirlwind of certifications, professional networking, and rediscovery was not just about skill-building. It was a turning point, a transformative phase that reshaped my understanding of achievement and growth. I had entered this period searching for stability and direction, but I emerged with so much more. The true value of accomplishments, I came to see, does not lie in applause or recognition from others. It is in the quiet strength we build along the way, the inner resilience that keeps us moving forward even when recognition feels out of reach.

During this time, I often reflected on the path I had taken. There were moments of doubt, times when I questioned whether all this effort was worth it. The HR conversation about the industry's preference for experience over education echoed in my mind. Instead of letting it discourage me, I chose to see it as a reminder that growth is deeply personal. It is about proving to yourself that you can rise to challenges, adapt to changing circumstances, and push past limits you once thought were fixed.

Each certification I pursued became a marker of my determination to grow. The Lean Six Sigma Black Belt was more than a course. It was a year-long commitment to mastering processes and learning to view problems with precision and clarity. The Train-the-Trainer course on the POSH Act felt deeply aligned with my values as I engaged with issues of equity and safety in the workplace. The mediation certification, requiring hours of study and practice, became a step toward becoming the kind of professional who could bridge divides and create meaningful resolutions.

Joining the real estate organization was another step that reignited my drive. What began as a networking opportunity became something much deeper. Interacting with senior developers from across the country reminded me of the respect and recognition that my work could inspire. Their encouragement reignited my confidence and validated my abilities in ways that felt deeply affirming. After years of quiet self-doubt, it was empowering to feel seen and valued once again.

What stood out most during this phase was how my idea of success evolved. It was no longer about titles, salaries, or external accolades. It was about the growth that comes from learning, adapting, and persevering. Every step forward, whether it was completing a certification, attending a workshop, or participating in a meaningful conversation with a peer, became a reminder of my capacity to keep going despite the challenges.

This phase also taught me patience, both with the process and with myself. I learned to accept that progress does not always look like a straight line. Some days felt like leaps forward, while others were quiet moments to reflect and regroup. I came to see value in both. Every challenge was an opportunity to test my resilience and expand my understanding of what I could accomplish.

As I stand here now, reflecting on that transformative time, I see that the real achievements of those years were not just the certifications or the networks I built. They were the lessons I learned about myself. I discovered that growth is not about external validation. It is about becoming the kind of person who can face uncertainty with courage, meet setbacks with determination, and greet success with humility. These lessons became the foundation for everything that followed, giving me the strength and clarity to move forward with unwavering purpose.

New Opportunities and Decisions Guided by Passion

Introducing myself as Dr. Kettaki Kasbekar is more than a title—it embodies a journey of grit, transformation, and boundless perseverance. Every time I attend a meeting or conference, people ask about my research, and I can see the genuine interest in their eyes. They're not just asking about the work itself; they're asking about the journey, about everything I went through to reach this point. And that reminder—of the battles I fought, of the nights I questioned myself—fuels me like nothing else.

One of my proudest moments came during an international conference focused on emerging technologies in business practices. Reviewing the conference theme, I felt compelled to contribute insights on leadership—a topic that resonates with me deeply. I poured my heart into crafting a paper titled Effective Leadership Strategies for Modern Organizations: A Management Perspective, drawing from years of experience, real-world challenges, and my own evolution as a leader. When I stepped up to present it, I was nervous yet excited. I felt that what I was sharing could genuinely make an impact, inspiring others to prioritize adaptability, inclusiveness, and a fresh outlook on innovation.

The response was overwhelming. I was honored with the Best Researcher Award—a recognition that went beyond the research itself, celebrating the heart and soul I'd put into my work. The cherry on top was seeing my paper published in a Scopus-indexed journal, a platform that would allow my ideas to reach people worldwide. It was a humbling experience, a reminder of how vital acknowledgment and encouragement are. They don't just validate our efforts; they ignite a renewed sense of purpose. It was these moments, these awards and recognitions, that kept me pushing, striving, and reaching.

Another turning point came during a conference in Delhi, where I met a real estate developer from Noida. We got into a deep, engrossing conversation about the industry's ethical standards, financial diligence, and the evolving expectations of corporate governance. It was an issue I had spent years studying, and there was a certain energy in our exchange—like we were both trying to solve a puzzle that mattered to both of us. At one point, he looked at me and said, "Why don't you consider becoming an independent director?"

That suggestion felt monumental. I had never thought about it in a serious way, but as he spoke, I could feel the potential in it. I knew that I had accumulated a wealth of experience and a firm commitment to ethical integrity, which would be invaluable in such a role. And with the flexible schedule I'd managed to build, I could actually make it work. Inspired, I dove into the certification process, studying the intricacies of corporate governance with a fierce dedication. And when I finally earned the certification, I felt like I'd stepped into a new chapter. Becoming a certified independent director wasn't just a line to add to my resume— it was a commitment to promoting transparency and responsibility, something I believed in wholeheartedly.

However, perhaps the most surprising opportunity came from an email from my GDBA mentor. I remember reading it and feeling a mix of excitement and disbelief. His friend, the owner of a major U.S. hotel chain, had been impressed by my research on customer relationship management. In fact, he was so taken with my work that he wanted me to join his leadership team as a CXO. My mind raced. A position like this could redefine my career! I could see the promise of financial growth, international exposure, and an exciting new field.

Yet, as exhilarating as the offer was, something held me back. Real estate wasn't just a career to me—it was woven into my very being. Over 25 years, it had become a part of who I was. Every land parcel, every new development, every project had left its mark on me. Real estate was where my heart was. I couldn't imagine spending my life in any other industry, no matter how enticing the role might be. I joined the call with my mentor's friend, intrigued but unsure. We had an excellent discussion, during which he commended my efforts and expressed his vision for the business. I informed him that I required time to reflect and consider the choice. Yet beneath it all, I understood. I realized that regardless of how life-changing the opportunity was, I couldn't abandon real estate. It wasn't merely a job—it was my mission, my enthusiasm, my essence.

Thus, I politely declined, filled with great respect and thankfulness, understanding I was selecting the route that matched my true self. I wasn't merely declining a job offer; I was embracing my vocation, the domain that had influenced me and that I, in return, wished to impact. Real estate is my true calling, and I experienced a profound, strong feeling of tranquility in making that choice.

At times, the toughest decisions bring us to our destined place, reminding us that achievement isn't defined by titles or wealth. It's about summoning the bravery to pursue your genuine passion, to heed that soft, unwavering voice inside.

Reflections on Success and the Road Ahead

Redefining Success and Embracing the Journey

When I think about the last 25 years in real estate, I don't see a seamless, perfect, and continual path to achievement. In what way can I do that? Achieving success has always been a bumpy journey. It resembles a collection of twisting routes—some guiding me to thrilling summits while others descending into unexpected valleys. Reflecting on the past, I realize that the situations I previously viewed as obstacles actually turned out to be instances of guidance, imparting wisdom that I wouldn't have gained otherwise.

And is that not indeed the essence of true success? A journey that is deeply personal and constantly evolving. Each bend and curve yielded something beneficial to me. On certain days, wisdom prevailed; on other days, strength was the driving force. However, each experience helped me to redefine my own definition of success, not based on others' standards. Transitioning into the real estate industry felt like entering unknown territory. I was not familiar with this field, but I understood the need to quickly adapt and learn. And I definitely learned. I learned that every difficulty presented an opportunity for personal growth, whether it involved handling legal disputes, nurturing client connections, or problem-solving in seemingly impossible situations. Certainly, there were times of uncertainty—wasn't that always the case? However, the joy of conquering those challenges justified all the effort.

Throughout all of my experiences, my passion for education has been the one constant that has kept me stable. From the time I was young, reading newspapers while having breakfast, I've always been curious to learn more. This passion did not diminish over time; it increased. To this day, I still can't go to bed without reading something - whether it's a research article, a fresh management strategy, or the most recent developments in the real estate industry. The continuous quest for knowledge has kept me relevant, curious, and strong. However, the reality is that it is not only important to stay up-to-date. It's all about progress. Each book, each article, and each course contributes to influencing my identity and my perspective on the world. Isn't that what life is all about? To continue learning, developing, and exploring?

Reflecting on this experience, I can't shake the thought of how crucial it is to establish our own definition of success, particularly for women in fields such as real estate, where conventional standards often determine our behavior and goals. It took me many years to understand that I was not obligated to adhere to the rules set by others. I had the potential to defy conventions, rely on my intuition, and forge a route that resonated with me. Such a freeing realization it was! For those of you at the beginning of your career or facing a decision point, I want to share a piece of advice I wish I had received: Success is not a one-size-fits-all concept. It's fine to create your own interpretation and to place importance on what is meaningful to you. To me, it was honesty, development, and a feeling of direction. What is your preference?

At certain times, my decisions were doubted by others. "Why do you behave this way?" they'd inquire. Why not choose the simpler path instead? However, deep down, I was confident that this path was meant for me, and the only doubter I had to convince was myself. Therefore, I trust that my story encourages you to have faith in yourself, to accept your abilities, and to always be unapologetically true to yourself. In the future, I envision a world where gender equality is not a goal we aim for but instead is the normal state of affairs. In an environment where both men and women are treated equally, all opinions are respected, and leadership mirrors the diversity of our society. Real estate plays a distinct role in shaping society, and I think its leaders should reflect the inclusivity and collaboration they want to promote in the world.

This is not only a career objective; it is also deeply personal. I desire for women in future generations to feel empowered, view themselves as leaders, and understand that their dreams are valid, regardless of how unconventional they may appear. Imagine the potential industries we could create by honoring all talents and viewpoints. There are infinite possibilities! Even after all this time, I still have the same passion for real estate as I did when I first began. Each project and each opportunity seems like a fresh journey. There is always more knowledge to acquire, more input to offer, and more goals to attain. Isn't that what makes life intriguing? Is the belief that the future holds better things ahead?

When I think about my favorite movie, Trishul, I see parallels to my own journey. The resilience, the determination to rise against all odds—it resonates deeply with me. Like the trident that symbolizes strength and victory, I carry those values into every phase of my life. Because no matter where the road takes me, I know one thing for sure: there's always another horizon to reach, another story to write.

Empowering the Next Generation and Championing Equality

Not long ago, I found myself sitting across from a 10-year-old boy at an orphanage—a child who had retreated into silence after failing his exams. He refused to eat, refused to engage in play, and had isolated himself from society. During one of my visits, the head of the orphanage expressed worry about their ability to help with the profound emotional challenges faced by the children due to their limited resources. I could observe the concern in his eyes, and my heart felt pain for this boy.

I chose to hang out with him, starting off with some quiet time, in the hopes of establishing a safe environment for him. Gradually, I urged him to open up about his emotions. It was a difficult experience as he felt scared, angry, and ashamed simultaneously. However, once he eventually expressed his feelings, a wave of emotion was unleashed, causing him to speak quickly and passionately about his frustrations and insecurities.

"I didn't pass," he stated, with tears filling his eyes. "Why bother attempting if I can't even pass?" His words landed on me with the force of a gut punch. I pondered the delicacy of young minds and how quickly they can perceive failure as a lasting identity. I comforted him softly, reassuring him, "Mistakes are not the conclusion; they are simply a detour along the way." Twists can result in exciting new routes. Leaving that day, I had a blend of emotions - a sense of relief that he was beginning to communicate and sadness at how challenging life seemed for someone so youthful. It brought back memories of a previous tragic event, when a close friend's son, a smart and talented young engineer, tried to take his own life due to job search difficulties. His parents and I were equally devastated. What caused his life to become so unbearable that he couldn't see other options?

The disaster lingered in my memory. It further solidified my belief: it is essential to educate the next generation to look past failure. In life, there are always alternative plans like Plan B, C, and D to fall back on if Plan A fails. Resilience is not only an inherent quality but also a capability that requires development and a mentality that should be cultivated in our children. Life's challenges can seem impossible to conquer if they are missing. These experiences have strengthened my determination to lead young minds, demonstrating that setbacks do not determine us but rather how we overcome them. And it's not just for future generations; it's for everyone, building a society that encourages development, even in times of unexpected challenges.

A lot of individuals inquire about my future plans, saying, "What comes after this, Kettaki?" Do you plan on remaining in the field of real estate? Are you going to concentrate on arbitration? Are you willing to commit to doing pro bono work or mentoring? Or perhaps consider investing in new business opportunities? To be honest, my response is consistently the same: Why not everything? Why would I restrict myself when my heart is overflowing with vitality, my mind filled with thoughts, and my spirit fueled by enthusiasm? Age is merely a numerical indication, a significant point along a broader chronological scale. If I possess the determination and energy to follow numerous aspirations, then why shouldn't I?

In my opinion, multitasking is not a chore but rather a gift. It is the ability to discover, generate, and engage in ways that are significant. Whether I am guiding a child, influencing the real estate field, or assuming leadership positions, I experience a feeling of purpose. And is not that the thing we all seek? Looking at the field I've dedicated myself to for many years, I envision a future that is more welcoming and diverse. A future in which women are not just included in the discussion but are prominent leaders in it. A future in which a variety of skills are valued and teamwork flourishes thanks to the distinctive viewpoints that each person offers. Real estate has the ability to establish this standard by focusing on shaping communities. However, it all begins with us - supporting equality, empowering voices, and guaranteeing that everyone is included.

This dream is not only a career goal for me; it is very meaningful on a personal level. I aspire to witness women entering boardrooms confidently, embracing leadership positions fearlessly, and understanding their worth in any environment they enter. I desire a world in which opportunities are defined by talent instead of gender, where diversity drives innovation and success, not just as a token gesture. As I keep moving forward, I realize that there is still a lot of work left to do. Every new obstacle presents an opportunity for personal development, while every relationship offers a chance to create a difference. When I help children face their fears, advocate for fairness in arbitration, or motivate women to pursue their dreams, I believe I am fulfilling my purpose.

To anyone who is curious about their ability to have an impact, the answer is yes, you can. Your contributions are important, whether they are in your field, your local area, or affecting just one individual. Together, we can create a world that is wealthier, more compassionate, and stronger for all. Let's welcome the twists in the road and forge new routes, as there is always another horizon ahead.

The Road Ahead: Passion, Purpose, and Restlessness

After years of striving, juggling countless responsibilities, and reaching milestones I once only dreamed of, I find myself with something unfamiliar: time. There's no impending deadline, no urgent task requiring my focus. Temporarily, it seems as if time has decelerated, yet instead of bringing tranquility, it awakens an unease within me. It feels strange, akin to a soldier coming back home following a lengthy and difficult battle. The soldier finds joy in his family's warmth, friends' laughter, and the familiarity of his surroundings. However, deep down, there remains a strong attraction, a gentle prompting saying, "The battlefield is calling. The war is not over yet."

This is my current feeling. Even though I appreciate the peace and quiet, it doesn't relax me—it motivates me, pushing me to pursue the next obstacle. The world is large, abundant with opportunities ready to be discovered, challenges ready to be overcome. Is there a way for me to ever come to a halt? How could I allow this flame inside me to fade?

A coworker recently told me, "Kettaki, you have put in a lot of effort and faced many challenges. The war has concluded. It is the moment to savor life-travel, unwind, and prioritize your own happiness." His words made me pause. He was correct; I've dedicated myself completely to all my endeavors. I have struggled on numerous fronts - personal, professional, and emotional. There is an attractive quality to taking a step back and allowing myself the freedom to just exist. However, as I pondered his words, I couldn't help but wonder: Does the struggle ever come to a definitive end?

Similar to a soldier, I have returned with both physical scars and tales to tell, as well as achievements and knowledge gained. However, while I enjoy reuniting with loved ones, a part of me is already longing for the next adventure. A restless soul never lets you find peace. It motivates you to expand, to contribute, and to accomplish greater things. Isn't that the essence of life? Isn't it the journey itself, rather than the destinations, that is, the thrilling, ongoing ascent towards something bigger? I could definitely decide to stop and enjoy life's more basic joys. I could explore different parts of the world, enjoy new adventures, and revel in the wonder of life without any responsibilities holding me back. And maybe I will, at times. However, I am aware deep down that I am not the type of person who can remain idle for an extended period of time. The fighter inside me finds fulfillment in purpose, in the excitement of resolving issues, and in the happiness of making a valuable contribution. The concept of remaining immobile seems unnatural, almost suffocating.

When individuals inquire about my future plans, I always respond with, "Why not pursue everything?" Am I interested in pursuing a career in the real estate industry? Yes. Am I interested in furthering my expertise in arbitration and mediation? Definitely. Am I interested in investing time in mentoring youth, offering free services, or delving into leadership positions? Why not? I view these not as different paths but as parts of the same road, connected by my passion and purpose. Age is frequently viewed as a restriction, a barrier that determines what is achievable and what is not. However, in my opinion, age is simply a numerical value with no additional significance. If I possess the energy, skills, and determination to create a positive impact, why should I hesitate? If anything, my past experiences have equipped me to accomplish more, to provide more, and to become more.

This stage of my life seems like a break - a short moment to think back, yet also to get ready for what comes next. Whether it's generating possibilities in the real estate sector, championing fairness, or mentoring the upcoming generation, I believe there is still plenty left to accomplish. And I'm prepared. Prepared for the obstacles, the hindrances, the victories, and the development. For me, life is not about being stagnant; it is about progress, growth, and meaning. I question if balance might be the solution. Maybe I can discover happiness in the small, joyful experiences of life, like travel, making memories, and appreciating the beauty around me, all while continuing to follow the passions that inspire me. Ultimately, life is not simply about deciding between rest and action; it involves combining the two, achieving balance amidst the chaos, and crafting a fulfilling and purposeful existence.

While contemplating how I've reached this point, I am filled with gratitude for all the lessons I've learned throughout my journey, not just for my accomplishments. I've come to understand that success is not about reaching a final goal but rather about the journey, the ongoing effort, the tireless quest for self-improvement and giving back. Every success, every challenge, and every instance of uncertainty has molded me into the person I am now. However, I am aware that this is not the final outcome. What could possibly be the case? The flame inside me continues to burn too strongly for me to quit at this point.

Indeed, at times, I ponder, have I put in sufficient effort? Have I successfully demonstrated what I intended to demonstrate? However, shortly after, another idea surfaced: How can I contribute further? That idea ignites me, rejuvenates me, and serves as a reminder that the most thrilling parts of my narrative have yet to be written. Life is not about remaining stationary and expecting the world to go on without you. It's about moving ahead, even when the road ahead is uncertain. It's all about moving with intention, enthusiasm, and the steadfast conviction that each step you make is important. Some could describe it as relentless. Some may perceive it as not needed. However, for me, this determination is not just a component of my identity—it is the fundamental core of living. I view my story as an unfinished book. It is a continuous sequence of developing sections, with each one expanding on the previous one, each one more profound, more significant, and more influential than the one preceding it.

Therefore, I welcome the unsettled feeling inside of me. I welcome the inquiries, the obstacles, and the unknown. Ultimately, it's not where I ultimately wind up that matters, but rather the journey I take to get there. It's important to value each moment, seize every opportunity, and make every effort count. As long as I possess the energy, the inquisitiveness, and the determination, I will continue to progress. I will continue to write my story, not only for my own benefit but also for those who will follow in my footsteps. Since life is a continuous journey, not a definite endpoint, my goal is to make each moment remarkable.

I have lost many things and opportunities in life, but I have gained much more in return. Some people believe that money is the most important thing, but for me, respect and gratitude hold far greater value. While some may think that degrees have little worth, there are still those who value education above everything else.

Author's Note

As I sit here writing to you, I can't help but feel a wave of emotions. This book is far more than just a compilation of stories from my life. It is my soul expressed in writing. It captures instances of victory and sorrow, periods when I questioned my abilities, and others when I felt invincible. It is the tale of a life experienced with enthusiasm, hardship, and the unwavering resolve to progress. I started my journey in real estate twenty-five years ago. I entered it with curiosity, some uncertainty, and a strong desire to learn. During that initial period, I had the privilege of working for leaders who motivated me. One of them had a talent for recognizing potential. I have witnessed structures emerge from empty plots of land and evolve into residences and areas where individuals make memories.

Real estate has always been my passion, and I've enjoyed witnessing communities develop from concepts into vibrant homes and workplaces. From locating the ideal parcel of land to delivering the keys to a delighted family, each aspect of the process is demanding yet fulfilling. There's nothing quite as special as witnessing the happiness on a person's face when they discover their dream of having a home has finally been fulfilled. However, like any journey that deserves to be taken, mine has encountered its fair share of difficult times. Being in a male-dominated sector presented unique difficulties. I've been overlooked in meetings, had my suggestions disregarded, and witnessed male coworkers claim recognition for projects I invested my passion into.

Errors and mistakes have also been a part of my story. I've been so devoted to my job that, at times, I let it dominate my life. I neglected my health, pushed through fatigue, and overlooked my own needs. I, too, faced challenges with workplace politics. I thought my efforts would be self-explanatory, but I discovered through experience that this isn't always true. Reflecting on the past, I realize how each experience influenced me. From joyful moments to periods of heartbreak, every experience has led me to a deeper understanding of my identity and my values. Real estate involves more than just structures. It focuses on individuals, connections, and establishing environments that realize dreams.

To the women reading this, I want to say something from the bottom of my heart. I know how it feels to be judged, overlooked, or underestimated. I've heard comments about women being too emotional to lead. I've had my contributions overlooked because of stereotypes that say women don't belong in certain spaces. But here is what I've learned. You do not need anyone's permission to belong. You are enough. Let's liberate ourselves from the expectations and judgments that restrict our progress. Let's take control of our decisions and embrace our achievements without any regrets. We are not limited by the roles that society gives us. We have the ability to craft our own narratives, and that carries significant power.

I'm not a celebrity or someone you've seen on the covers of magazines. I'm just a woman who has walked through life with determination and a deep desire to do something meaningful. This isn't a book about fame or success. It's about strength, about those quiet battles we face when no one is looking. Life doesn't hand you a guidebook, and there were times when I had to make tough decisions without knowing the outcome. I'll admit there are personal moments I've chosen not to share here, moments that shattered me to my core. Those aren't the focus of this book because I've never wanted sympathy. My purpose is to show you that no matter what life throws at you, even when it feels like thunderballs raining down, you can stand strong. You can choose not to let the storms define your path.

This book tells my story, yet it also speaks to anyone who has encountered difficulties and continued to push ahead. Life will consistently present its highs and lows, yet each setback, every success, and all lessons are significant. I hope you feel motivated to accept your own path as you read through these pages. Continue pushing forward, regardless of how difficult it appears. The perspective from the opposite side is worthwhile. Life might not always unfold as you intended, yet it has a tendency to astonish you. In times of uncertainty, keep this in mind, you possess the ability to achieve much more than you realize. Make that jump. Have confidence in yourself. And never allow fear to stop you.